LONDON'S HIDDEN BURIAL GROUNDS

Robert Bard and Adrian Miles

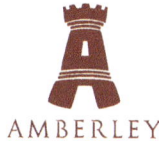

AMBERLEY

First published 2017

Amberley Publishing
The Hill, Stroud
Gloucestershire, GL5 4EP

www.amberley-books.com

Copyright © Robert Bard and Adrian Miles, 2017

The right of Robert Bard and Adrian Miles to be identified as the Authors of this work has been asserted in accordance with the Copyrights, Designs and Patents Act 1988.

All rights reserved. No part of this book may be reprinted or reproduced or utilised in any form or by any electronic, mechanical or other means, now known or hereafter invented, including photocopying and recording, or in any information storage or retrieval system, without the permission in writing from the Publishers.

British Library Cataloguing in Publication Data.
A catalogue record for this book is available from the British Library.

ISBN 978 1 4456 6111 7 (print)
ISBN 978 1 4456 6112 4 (ebook)

Origination by Amberley Publishing.
Printed in Great Britain.

Contents

	Introduction	4
1.	Death in Dickens's London	9
2.	Plague Pits and Pest Fields	13
3.	London's Worst Nineteenth-Century Burial Grounds	33
4.	Disused and Hidden Jewish Burial Grounds	85
	Bibliography	94

Introduction

It is a fascinating thought that many hundreds of generations of Londoners lie beneath the city as we know it. Throughout the millennia, burial grounds have been developed, built over, and forgotten. Occasionally, when modern development takes place, the remains of Londoners past are disturbed and we are reminded of a London that has long since disappeared. This hidden aspect of London has been remarked upon since the London historian Stow, writing at the end of the sixteenth century, commented on bones that were unearthed in 1576 at Spitalfields.

The digging of many of the railway lines and tube tunnels led to the disturbing of previously unknown burial grounds, right through from Roman times to the present day, such as the recent Crossrail project. The recognition of the importance of post-medieval burials in recent times has led to much more archaeological excavation of burial grounds, when their sites have come up for development, which has vastly increased our knowledge of the burial grounds and the practices that went on within them.

The knowledge that there is an untold history, which lies often forgotten under our feet, has fascinated generations of those that have recorded London's history. Indeed, in the 1880s a Mrs Holmes observed: 'In looking one day at Rocque's plan of London (1742–5) I noticed how many burial-grounds and churchyards were marked upon it which no longer existed...I commenced to draw up a list of all the burying-places, of which I could find any record, still existing, or that had ever existed in London. It was no easy task.'[1] By the use of 'ancient and modern maps' and visiting the many sites she identified such as 'the German ground in the Savoy, the additional ground to St Martins in the Fields, and Thomas' ground in Golden Lane...' all of which had disappeared. As a middle-class Victorian woman, she tells us that she had some fascinating experiences while out 'graveyards-hunting'. Twice she had mud thrown at her: 'once by a woman in Cable Street...and once by a man in Silchester Road'. At the time, with research at the British Museum and the use of sixty Ordnance Survey maps, Holmes identified within the 'County and City of London' 362 burial grounds, of which forty-one were still in use. A further ninety had become public gardens and playgrounds. This number excluded churches and chapels with vaults under them. Thus began an extensive work which looked at all categories of burial grounds ranging from Roman burial grounds to 'Pest-Fields and Plague Pits' and many more. The end result of this extensive

---

1 Holmes, I. M. (1896). *The London Burial Grounds. Notes on Their History from the Earliest Times to the Present Day* ... Illustrated, London, T. F. Unwin. p.xxx

survey was a 'List of Burial-Grounds in Existence' and 'Burial-Grounds which have disappeared'. Holmes identifies a cycle of use relating to burial grounds that still holds true when she says that

> it is interesting to trace on maps of different dates the rise and fall of a graveyard. First there is the actual field, which on some particular day was acquired for the purpose. Then there is the burial-ground formed and in use. Then the plot appears to be vacant – put to no purpose, or used as a yard. Lastly buildings are on it, and the graveyard has quite disappeared.[2]

Holmes's survey was used by the Metropolitan Public Gardens Association, whose principal objective was the protection, preservation, safeguarding and acquiring for the permanent preservation and the public use of, among other things, disused burial grounds and churchyards.

Holmes followed on from a publication by Dr George Alfred Walker, who was disgusted by the unhygienic and overcrowded state on many of London's churchyards and burial grounds. The report he wrote consists of many first-hand accounts of not only the state of some of these grounds, but the appalling practices that were often carried out by the owners of the many private chapels and grounds, which involved the destruction of newly buried coffins and mortal remains in order to cram more dead into the same piece of ground.

Walker, a surgeon, was to become a prominent campaigner against burials within areas of dense human habitation. Walker's surgery was located at No. 101 Drury Lane, close to the St Martin's Drury Lane burial ground, a ground so overflowing with bodies that the graveyard became 'level with the first floor windows surrounding the place'.[3] Walker, against much vested opposition, believed that the emanations coming from London's overcrowded burial grounds were dangerous to the health of those who lived in the vicinity. The flavour of Walker's style can be gained from the introduction to his magnificently titled 1846 document 'Spa-Fields Golgotha, Last Fire at the Bone-House in the Spa-Fields Golgotha, or, The Minute Anatomy of Grave-Digging'. Walker quotes another Doctor and begins:

> No burying-places should be tolerated within cities or towns, much less in or about CHURCHES and CHAPELS. This custom is excessively injurious to the inhabitants, and especially to those who frequent public worship in such CHAPELS and CHURCHES. God, decency and health forbid this shocking abomination *** From long observation I can attest that CHURCHES and CHAPELS situated in grave-yards, and those especially within whose walls the dead are interred, are perfectly unwholesome; and many, by attending such places, are shortening their passage to the house appointed for the living. What increases the iniquity of this abominable and deadly work is, that the burying-grounds attached to many CHURCHES and

---

2   Holmes, p.20
3   Walker, *Gatherings from Graveyards*, p.162

CHAPELS are made a source of PRIVATE GAIN. The whole of this preposterous conduct is as indecorous and unhealthy as it is profane.[4]

Spa Fields, located in Islington, was one of London's most notoriously overcrowded private burial grounds. The site has a haunting atmosphere and can still be visited.

The scars on the London landscape of the grounds and events described by both Walker and Holmes are still clear to be seen in the playgrounds of schools, many of which were built over and beside these burial grounds, and in the hidden nooks and crannies of central London where a surprisingly large number of people live in proximity to these unmarked grounds – without realising the meaning of the hillocks and lumps in the ground on their doorsteps. The majority of those interred up until modern times had no gravestone or marker. Many burial grounds are still not built on, but are preserved as courtyards to council flats and act as gardens to rows of houses. Some are quite obvious when looking specifically for a disused or forgotten place of interment, but the majority need a sharp eye and a copy of an eighteenth- or nineteenth-century map to locate. A surprisingly large part of central London and the suburbs still retain the same road names and outlines as when depicted 250 or more years ago.

The Black Death in 1349 had a profound effect on the need to allocate large areas of land for burials. The plague of 1665, with deaths at one stage running at 4,000 persons per week, put extraordinary pressure on churchyards, leading to overflowing and highly unsanitary conditions. This pressure led to the creation of new burial grounds, one of which was the Dissenter's ground Bunhill Fields, which was not completed until 1666. There is some dispute as to whether the ground was actually used for plague burials, but the result for twenty-first-century London is an interesting burial ground, which contains the remains of some of London's better-known citizens. In the nineteenth century, development in the area of Marble Arch, particularly Connaught Place and Bryanston Street, led to the unearthing of many human remains. The workmen had recovered some of the many thousands of victims of the Tyburn Gallows who had been buried in pits opened up alongside the gallows to receive their remains. Somewhere near the corner of Oxford Street and the Edgware Road lie the remains of three of the regicides responsible for the execution of Charles I, including Oliver Cromwell.

The concern over the public health risks posed by overcrowded urban burial grounds resulted in the 1852 Burial Act, which led to their closure through 1853–54.

Many of London's burial grounds now survive as City of London gardens. Holmes, writing in the 1890s, tell us, for example, that the burial ground of 'the priory of St.Augustine Papey survives in the little churchyard of St.Martin Outwich in Camomile Street, on the corner of Threadneedle Street and Bishopsgate, which was presented to the parish by Robert Hyde in 1538. A surprisingly large number of closed burial grounds were turned into children's playgrounds and schoolyards, and many of them remain so today.

---

4   Walker, G. A. (1846). Burial-ground Incendiarism. The last fire at the Bone-House in the Spa-Fields Golgotha, or the minute anatomy of Grave-digging in London, London. Intro p.1

An Unhealthy Stench

The result of the shortage of burial space and the overflowing churchyards was that burials were shallow and often haphazard. Appalling descriptions abound of the stench emanating from under the floors of churches, around the churchyards, and in some cases schools, which had vaults crammed with remains directly underneath. The perceived hazard to health was such that Parliament stepped in with statutes relating to burials. It was during the period between the 1840s and the 1870s that increasing use was made of dedicated burial grounds on the periphery of London that were not related to specific churches. These new burial grounds were often designed as gardens and many are now centres for tourism in their own right. Kensal Green Cemetery opened in January of 1833. Highgate Cemetery opened in 1839. Bunhill Fields, the former seventeenth-century Dissenter's Burial Ground and the last resting place of approximately 120,000 Londoners, including William Blake, John Bunyan and Daniel Defoe, became a public open space in 1867. The protests and campaigns against the state of London's burial grounds, stimulated by serious cholera outbreaks, resulted in a series of acts that started with the 1852 Metropolitan Burial Act, which brought an end to burials in central London.

Outside of the mass hurried burials of the centuries in which London was afflicted by the plague, most burials were part of a personal or family tragedy. It is difficult to comprehend when reading Walker and Holmes how haphazard and indifferent many of these interments were. In the twenty-first century, where death is clinical, and mostly followed through in a business-like and respectful manner, nineteenth-century passers-by of some of London's better-known churches could be witness to churchyards littered with scraps of coffins and decaying human remains. St Mary's Church on Whitechapel Road, which now survives as a white marked outline in the grass surrounded by a scattering of tombstones, was described in 1839 by Walker as abutting 'upon one of the greatest thoroughfares in London…its appearance altogether is extremely disgusting, and I have no doubt that the putrefactive process which is here very rapidly going on, must, in a great measure, be the cause of producing, certainly of increasing, the numerous diseases by which the lower order of the inhabitants of this parish have so frequently been visited'. He continues painting a picture that seems almost unimaginable when walking through the remains of the ground today: 'The ground is so densely crowded as to present one entire mass of human bones and putrefaction', which are in the course of further interments 'exhumed by the shovelfuls, and disgustingly exposed to the pensive observations of the passer-by ---to the jeers or contempt of the profane or brutal…most of the graves are very shallow, --some entire coffins, indeed, are to be found within a foot and a half of the surface.'[5] The East End of London was by no means atypical. Venues such as St Anne's, Soho, boasted churchyards where graves were kept open in 'expectancy' and Walker reports that 'rotten coffin wood and fragments of are scattered about'.[6] Even churchyards such as that of St Margaret's in Westminster, which lies adjacent to Westminster Abbey, and today presents a picture of cultivated greenery and

---

5   Walker p.168
6   Walker p.177

propriety, caused disquiet and was full to saturation point. Sir Edwin Chadwick, public health commissioner between 1848 and 1854 carried out a burial ground survey in 1841:

> Again, where the drainage of the district in which the church may be placed is of an inferior description, and liable to be impeded periodically by the state of the tide, as in the vicinity of the Houses of Parliament, where all the drains are closed at high water, the atmosphere is frequently of the most inferior quality. I am fully satisfied, for instance, not only from my own observation, but from different statements that have reached me, and also from the observations of parties who have repeatedly examined the subject at my request, that the state of the burying-ground around St. Margaret's church is prejudicial to the air supplied at the Houses of Parliament, and also to the whole neighbourhood. One of them, indeed, stated to me lately that he had avoided the churchyard for the last six months, in consequence of the effects he experienced the last time he visited it. These offensive emanations have been noticed at all hours of the night and morning; and even during the day the smell of the churchyard has been considered to have reached the vaults in the House of Commons, and traced to sewers in its immediate vicinity. [7]

The constant burials-upon-burials dramatically raised the level of the churchyards. A consequence of these burials was contamination of the drinking water. Many churchyards had water pumps, which aided the spread of disease.

Equally interesting are the less obvious remnants of London's burial grounds. Numerous grounds have disappeared under the combined advance of railway extensions and office blocks. Many partly remain as recreation grounds, with parts under adjoining schools or car parks. It is clear that Holmes' 1896 observation that many burial grounds now lay under schools and playgrounds still holds true. It is likely that rather than face the problem and cost of mass exhumations associated with redevelopment, the simple alternative after the closure of the metropolitan burial grounds in the 1850s was to turn them into recreation or playgrounds. Every foray into the centre and suburbs of London, armed with a copy of Mrs Holmes' book and printed-out sections of maps from earlier centuries, provided surprises. Aldgate Churchyard, the site of one of London's largest plague pits, and the place where two gravediggers died in 1838 from inhaling the noxious fumes of putrefaction while digging a burial pit, can be imagined from the distance of the twenty-first century, despite the now truncated nature of the Aldgate Church burial area. Many of the lost burial grounds retain an atmosphere of their pasts. Many of our forebears lie completely forgotten in unmarked graves or in unmarked grounds, now totally forgotten. Some lie in the unlikeliest of places. The Aske's Hospital Burial Ground in Great Chart Street, Hoxton, is situated in the courtyard of a block of council flats. The overflow ground for St Mary's Church in Whitechapel lies just behind Whitechapel Road on a housing estate. The only reminder of its past is the height of the ground above the surrounding houses, and the ominous dips and humps in the ground.

---

7 Chadwick, E. (1845). A report on the results of a special inquiry into the practice of interment in towns, etc., by C. Sherman. P. 41

1. Death in Dickens's London

Sickening and Horrible

Charles Knight, a mid-nineteenth-century London historian[8] devotes an entire chapter to what was then an extremely topical subject, the burials in London and the overcrowding that had developed to a stage where health was considered to be endangered. He introduces his subject:

> It was on the 8th of March, 1842, that the Committee of the House of Commons was appointed, to which we are indebted for the discovery of a state of things in London which is truly described by one witness as 'sickening' and 'horrible', and which exhibits England, through its capital (in the words of the Committee's Report), as an 'instance of the most wealthy, moral, and civilised community in the world, tolerating a practice and an abuse which has been corrected for years by nearly all other civilised nations in every part of the globe.[9]

Sir Edwin Chadwick presented a picture that although bad, was made worse by the increasing number of private entrepreneurs who, in the cause of profit, set up burial grounds which catered to the poor. In his report to the House of Commons he wrote:

> The most crowded burial grounds, on the average, are, it appears, the grounds which belong to private individuals, usually undertakers. In these places an uneducated man generally acts as minister, puts on a surplice, and reads the church service, or any other service that may be called for. These grounds are morally offensive, and appear to be physically dangerous in proportion to the numbers interred in them. In one of them the numbers interred appears to be at the rate of more than 2,300 per acre per annum. Names are given to these places by the owners, importing connexion with congregations, but without any apparent authority for doing so…[10]

The result of these privatised burial yards was, as Chadwick reports, that 'in the common grave-yards in the metropolis, the bones are scattered about or wheeled away

---

8 Knight, C. (1841). London. Charles Knight & Co. Vol.3 1851 ed. p.168
9 Knight p.166
10 Chadwick p.134

to a bone-house, where they are thrown in a heap'.[11] Witnesses were called and the report contains some of their evidence. The report of Dr Lyon Playfair makes grim reading:

> I know several church-yards from which most foetid smells are evolved, and gases with similar odour are emitted...The worst burying grounds which have come under my notice are those belonging to private persons, generally undertakers, who make their livelihood by interring at a cheap rate. I visited one of these only a few days since. It was about 150 feet long and about 30 broad, and had been used for 80 years as a burying ground, and was still a favourite place of interment among the poor. Of course many bodies are placed in one grave, and when the ground becomes too much raised by bodies, it is levelled, and the boxes, &c., exhumed during the levelling, are thrown into a large cellar fitted to receive them. This whole ground was a mass of corruption, as well may be supposed, and it is situated in a densely populated neighbourhood. I mention this case as one among many other similar cases of private burying grounds, in order to suggest that attention should be paid in any alteration respecting the laws regulating interments, to prevent burying-grounds being kept as objects of pecuniary speculation, at least within towns; for this practice gives much inducement to violate every feeling of decency and regard for public health in the desire for gain.[12]

Profit of Death

In the cause of private gain, little was sacrosanct. The sanctity and finality of death came a distant second in consideration to the financial rewards associated with interment. The English church relied on burial fees to maintain the clergy, as did the Nonconformist clergy. The private burial ground proprietors saw Walker as a direct threat; in all Walker was heavily opposed. He concentrated on bringing a small number of particularly notorious burial grounds to the fore to promote his case for burials outside of London. These grounds were Spa-Fields in Islington, the Enon Chapel in Clements Lane, now under the London School of Economics, and the neighbouring oddly named 'Green Ground' in Portugal Street, now partly under the LSE Library.

These private grounds were not consecrated, and the lack of solemnity and decorum when providing the poorer sorts with interment became a matter of scandal, a matter on which Chadwick felt compelled to comment:

> On occasions of several interments taking place in burial-grounds in the metropolis at the same time, the master undertakers will volunteer their services to get the crowd of by-standers into some order, and show how much might be done by other and better superintendence to add to the impressiveness of the last scene. The inferior attendants,

---

[11] Chadwick p.137
[12] Chadwick p.138

the grave-diggers, at the interments which I have witnessed at the new cemeteries, attended, as they usually do at the parochial grounds, in a disorderly condition – unshaven, dirty in person, in dirty shirts and in the old and the common filthy dress. During the burial service the undertakers' men only concerned themselves in removing the feathers from the hearse and preparing for an immediate return; all the attendants began talking on other matters, and went their different ways immediately the coffin was lowered; the mourners were left with the utmost unconcern, except by the grave-diggers, who followed them in the attitude of the usual solicitations of money for drink.[13]

The practice of removing coffins almost immediately after a burial and chopping those up to make room for more corpses in an area of limited space was very common. Often the coffins may have only lain in the ground for a matter of days or weeks. There were many London churchyards and private burial grounds where the remnants of coffins could be seen scattered around. Of these practices Knight comments that they

have taken place at Enon Chapel, the Globe Fields, St. Andrew's Undershaft, St. Anne's, Soho (where the wonderful man Fox did not mind cutting through a body buried but three weeks), St. Clement's churchyard, St. Clement Danes, St. Martin's in the Fields (Drury Lane), St. Mary's, Vinegar Yard—in short, at so many places that it is far from improbable that the greater part of London grave-yards have witnessed similar scenes. Among the minor practices of the grave-yard gentry, may he mentioned the interring bodies at insufficient depth when they happened to be in an idle mood, and then, when it became necessary to turn the spot to the best advantage, of digging the coffins up, and re-burying them at the suitable depth. From a similar motive, when a deep grave has been dug, it appears that it is sometimes allowed to remain open till it is filled, boards and earth being merely placed over the top. At the grave-yard in Drury Lane they gradually waxed so confident in this habit, that even when the unhappy relatives said they did not like to go away without seeing the grave filled up, they pertinaciously refused.

Dickensian Gloom

Charles Dickens has conveyed some of the atmosphere and the squalor that were common to many London churchyards in the early to mid-nineteenth century. Certain scenes from *Bleak House* are often quoted as typifying the gloomy dankness of mid-Victorian London graveyards:

At last we stood under a dark and miserable covered way, where one lamp was burning over an iron gate and where the morning faintly struggled in. The gate was closed. Beyond it was a burial ground – a dreadful spot in which the night was very slowly stirring, but where I could see heaps of dishonoured graves and stones,

---

13 Chadwick p.140

hemmed in by filthy houses with a few dull lights in their windows and on whose walls a thick humidity broke out like a disease.[14]

There have been scholarly attempts to locate some of the churchyards which he vividly described, and omitted to name. It is contended that the *Bleak House* character 'Poor Jo' London Churchyard has been identified by virtue of a letter that Dickens had written from Boston on 4 April 1868:

> Convey yourself back to London by the agency of that powerful Locomotive, your imagination, and walk through the centre avenue of Covent Garden Market from West to East:– that is to say, with your back towards the church, and your face towards Drury Lane Theatre. Keep straight on along the side of the Theatre, and about halfway down, on the left side of the way, behind the houses, is a closely hemmed in grave-yard – happily long disused and closed by the Law. I do not remember that the grave-yard is accessible from the street now, but when I was a boy it was to be got at by a low covered passage under a house, and was guarded by a rusty iron gate. In that churchyard I long afterwards buried the 'Nemo' of Bleak House.[15]

It was of this Drury Lane burial ground that George Walker in his 1839 volume *Gatherings from Grave Yards* had written that

> many thousands of bodies have been here deposited. The substratum was, some years since, so saturated with dead, that the place 'was shut up' for a period. The ground was subsequently raised to its present height – *level with the first floor windows surrounding the place*, and in this superstratum vast numbers of bodies have, up to this period, been deposited. A short time since a pit was dug (a very common practice here) in one corner of the ground; in it many bodies were deposited at different periods, the top of the pit being covered only with boards. This ground is a most intolerable and highly dangerous nuisance to the entire neighbourhood. Rather more than two years ago, in making three areas to the centre houses on the western side of this burying ground, many bodies were disturbed and mutilated; the inhabitants of the houses frequently annoyed by the most disgusting and repulsive sights. (pp 162-163)

---

14 Dickens, Bleak House, chapter 14
15 Trevor Blount. The Graveyard Satire of Bleak House in the Context of 1850.The Review of English Studies, New Series, Vol.14, No.56 (Nov,1963),p.370

2. Plague Pits and Pest Fields

Legacy of the Black Death and Plague

The Black Death of 1349 and Plague of 1665 in particular have created their own brand of London burial mythology. Scarcely do workmen strike disordered or scattered human remains, not an uncommon occurrence in central London, than there is a presumption that the site must be a 'plague pit'. The mythology currently revolves around diverted tube lines, patches of land in prime areas not built on, such as Knightsbridge Green, and the increasingly popular genre of 'ghosts of the London underground', many of which are associated with the disturbance of the dead during construction of underground and railway tunnels. Vanessa Harding, an authority on such burials, comments that 'the site of any discovery of plentiful human remains

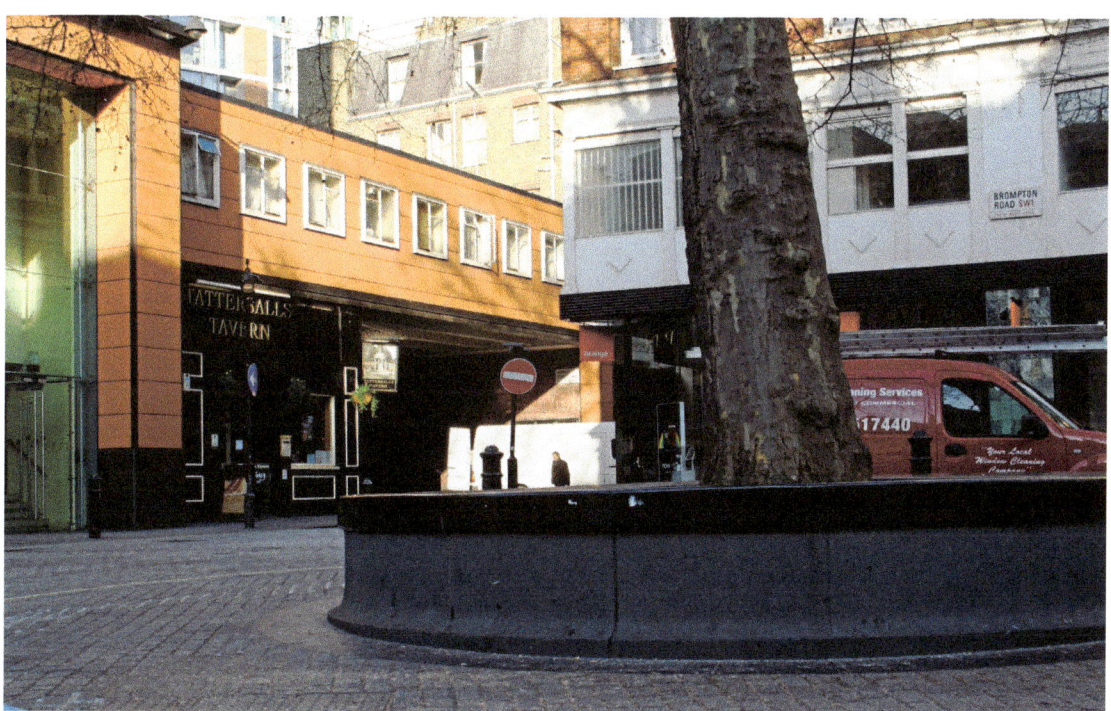

Holmes, 1896, describes this burial ground as being for 'victims of the plague from the leper hospital ... A grassy, closed triangle opposite Tattersals'. The Tattersals Tavern, back left, is a reminder. (Photograph by the author)

in a location no longer used for burial tends to be identified as a plague pit, unless a more reliable history is quickly attached to it. There were undoubtedly some temporary and irregular plague burial sites, but though few are well documented, their overall number may have been quite limited'.[16] Individual church records often refer to plague burials in their churchyards, and some contemporary witnesses who have recorded their experiences such as Pepys and Evelyn, along with Defoe's 1722 fictional account, give us an idea of where to look for these sites. Many of the burial pits were actually located in churchyards and in some, such as Stepney, where the area is railed off for dog walking, the grounds can still be identified. A number of these burial sites, which will be looked at individually, are still traceable in the form of raised churchyards, but just as many lie under modern car parks, playgrounds, and office buildings.

Black Death Burials 1348
Charterhouse

The London Charterhouse was founded by Sir Walter Manny in 1371. It was situated on sparsely populated land immediately outside the city walls, in the immediate vicinity of Smithfield Market, and thrived as a monastic institution until the Reformation. It was 'suppressed' in 1538. There were three Black Death burial grounds created at the Charterhouse as the London churchyards began to fill. The cemetery to the north was known originally as 'Nomannesland' and was founded in 1348 by the Bishop of London, Ralph de Stratford. It was later known as the Pardon Churchyard (not to be confused with that near St Paul's). Stow comments on Pardon Churchyard that, at the time of writing at end of the sixteenth century, it 'severed for burying of such as desperately ended their lives, or were executed for felonies, who were fetched thither usually in a close cart...'[17] It is probable that this cemetery was situated between Great Sutton Street and the south side of Clerkenwell Road. The cemetery to the south, which covers a large part of Charterhouse Square, was founded shortly afterwards, either at the end of 1348 or beginning of 1349. This cemetery lay within the area of 'Spitalcroft' and lay within land leased from St Bartholomew's Hospital.[18] A Museum of London Archaeology (MOLA) volume on Charterhouse estimates that in these combined (West Smithfield) cemeteries there are around 10,000 bodies. (Barber and Thomas, 2002.)

This area of 'no man's land' subsequently became known as the Pardon Churchyard, which was used for suicides and executed felons. Mrs Holmes (1896) identifies the site of this burial ground as

---

16 Epidemic Disease in London, ed. J.A.I. Champion (Centre for Metropolitan History Working Papers Series, No. 1, 1993), pp. 53-64

17 Stow p.362

18 See Thomas, C. J., B. Sloane, et al. (1997). Excavations at the Priory and Hospital of St Mary Spital, London. London, Museum of London Archaeology Service. pp.12-15

Wilderness Row, now merged into Clerkenwell Road...while the gardens and courts of the Charterhouse, the Square, the site of a demolished burial-ground for the pensioners (Sutton's Ground), and the burial-ground which still exists at the northern end of the precincts, are all part of the Spittle Croft and of the monastery burial ground...the 'Victualling-office', [for the Charterhouse] which took the place of St. Mary's Abbey, was where the Royal Mint at present stands, and ... the abbey graveyard was where the entrance courtyard is now.[19]

An article in *Notes and Queries* of 2 July 1853 reads:

When the ground in Charterhouse Square was opened in 1834, for the purposes of sewerage (I believe), vast numbers of bones and skeletons were found, being the remains, as was supposed, of those who died of the Plague in 1348, and had been interred in that spot, as forming a part of Pardon Churchyard, which had lately been purchased by Sir Walter Manny, for the purposes of burial, and attached to the Carthusian convent there.

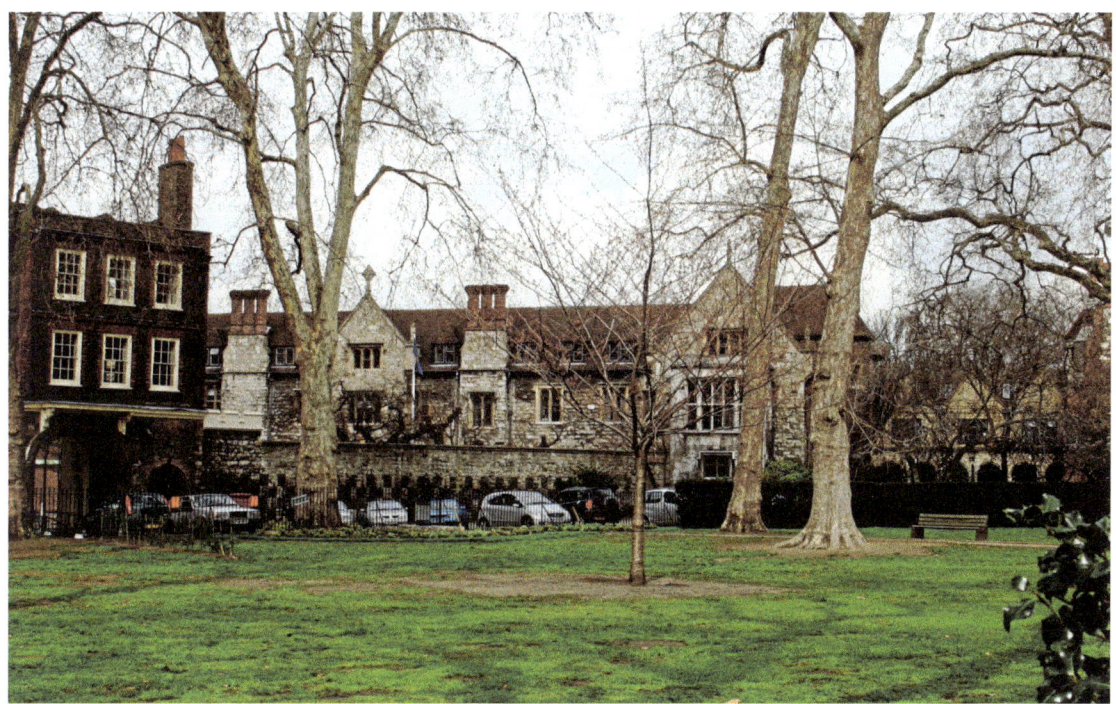

'When the ground in Charterhouse Square was opened in 1834, for the purposes of sewerage ... vast numbers of bones and skeletons were found...' Charterhouse Square. (Photograph by R. Bard)

---

19 Holmes, *The London Burial Grounds*, p.120

When in March 2000 some human remains were found on the site of Nos 35–42 Clerkenwell Road, the Museum of London Archaeology stated that this was:

> probably evidence of the location of the Pardon Churchyard, documented from the 14th century and originally designated for the burial of victims of the Black Death. At least five individuals were identified during excavation for drains and manholes. (Site code CKE00, London Archaeologist Round-up 2000)

A third Black Death cemetery was located at East Smithfield, on the site of the former Royal Mint, close to the Tower of London. Holmes states that 'the Victualling-office', which took the place of St.Mary's Abbey, was where the Royal Mint at present stands, and …the abbey graveyard was where the entrance courtyard is now'.

Spitalfields

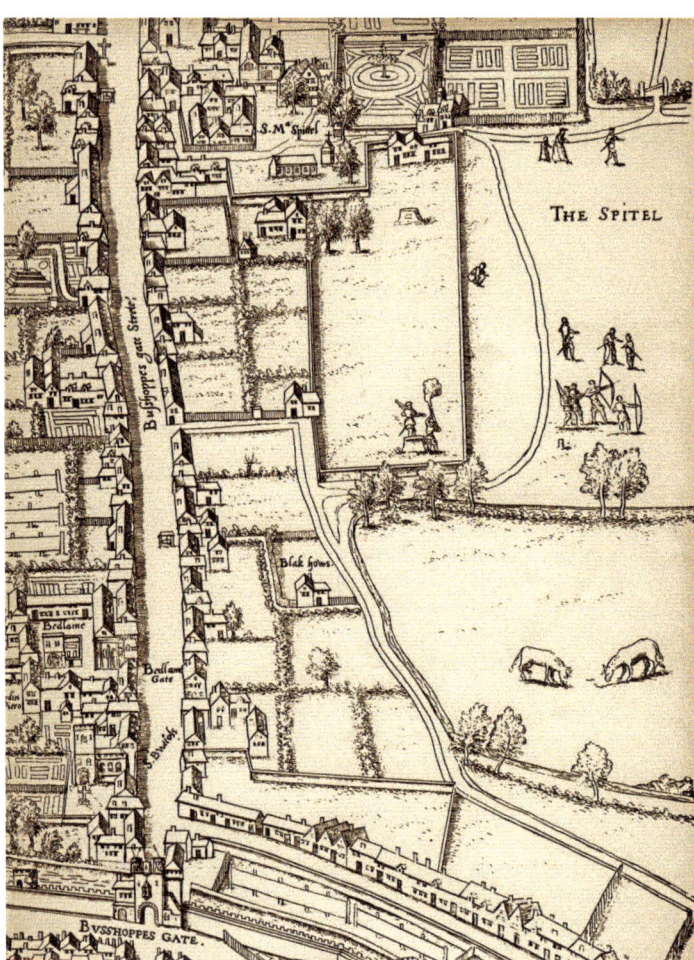

Agas Map 1562/3 showing the rural nature of Spitalfields in the sixteenth century. St Mary 'Spitel' can be seen top left to the east of Bishopsgate Street.

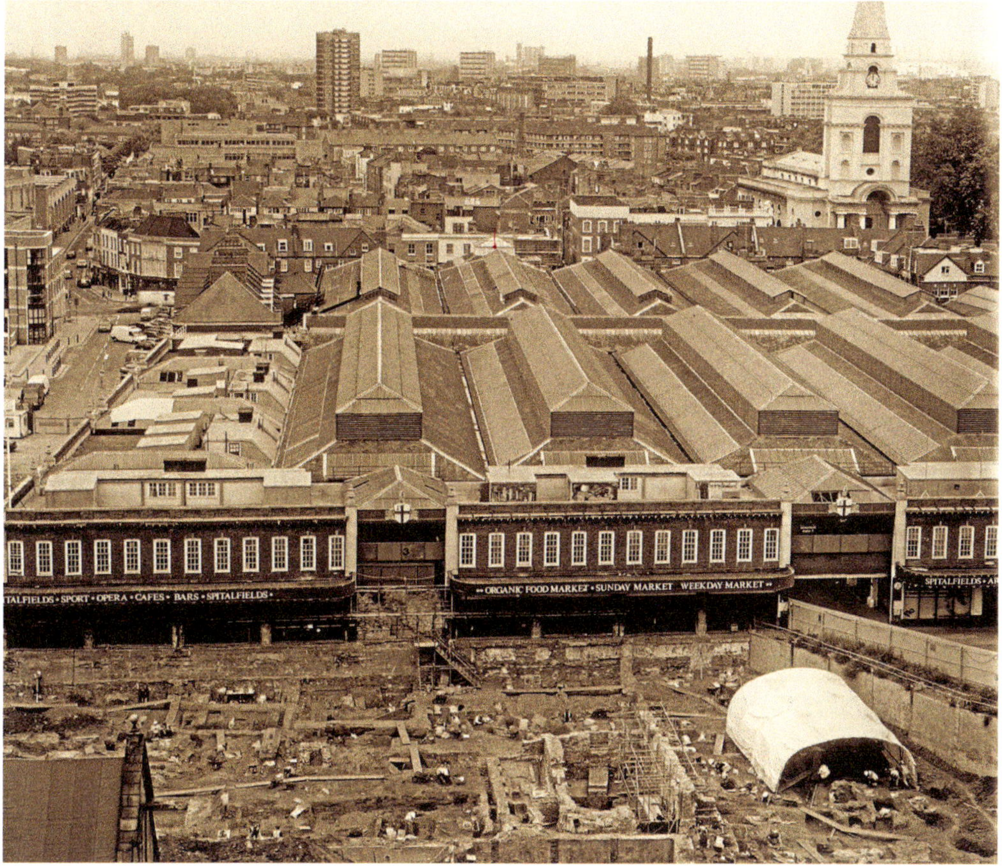

Excavations at Spitalfields with the market in the immediate background, and Christ Church in the background to the right. (*Life and Death in London's East End: 2000 Years at Spitalfields*)

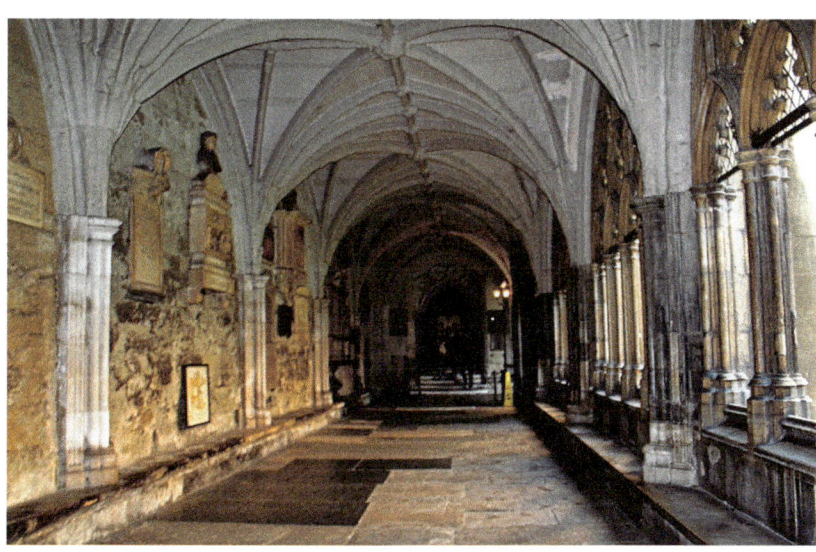

The north walk of the cloister area, Westminster Abbey, where twenty-six monks who perished from the Black Death were buried in a single grave. (Photograph by R. Bard)

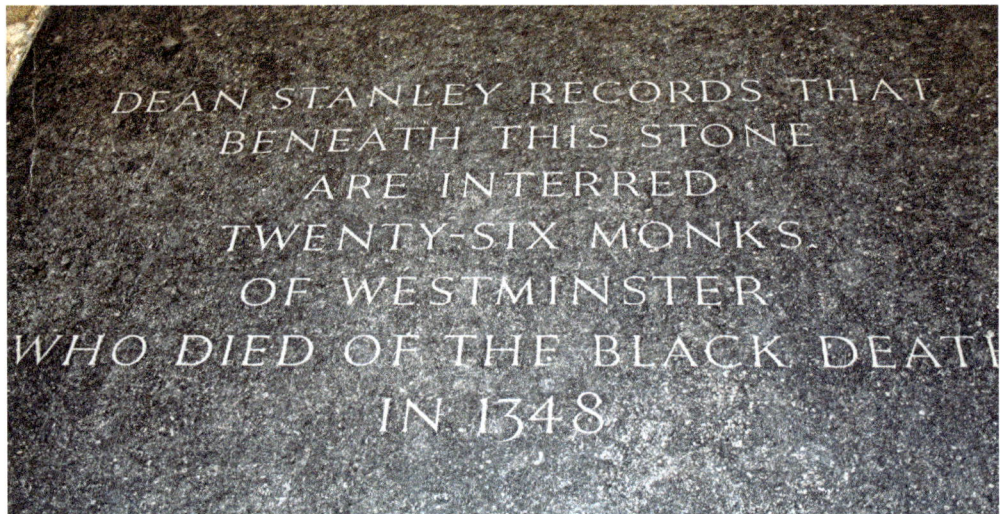

A close-up of the Black Death grave in Westminster Abbey.

Westminster Abbey

The events of 1348/9 are apparent in the north walk of the cloister area of Westminster Abbey.

Echoes of the 1665 Plague

Such was the impact of this deadly disease, which changed the landscape of central London, that the scars of mass burials can still be seen over 350 years later.

> When deaths became so numerous, the church-yards were unable to contain the bodies, and the usual modes of interment were no longer observed: occasional pits of great capacity were dug in several parts, to which the dead were brought by cartloads, collected by the ring of a bell, and the doleful cry of Bring out your dead! They were put into the carts with no other covering than rugs or sheets tied round them by their friends, if they had any surviving; and were shot down in promiscuous heaps! Sometimes the drivers of these carts would drop in their employments, and the carts would be found without any conductor; in the parish of Stepney it was said they lost within the year, 116 sextons, grave-diggers, and their assistants![20]

The historian Noorthouck observes that under the orders of Earl Craven and the other justices of Westminster 'the churchyards [were] covered two feet thick with fresh earth; to prevent as far as possible any revival of the pestilential taint'.[21]

---

20 Noorthouck Book 1, Ch. 14: From the Restoration to the Fire', A New History of London: Including Westminster and Southwark (1773), pp. 210-230

21 Ibid pp.210-230

> The distemper sweeping away such multitudes as I have observed, many, if not all the out-parishes were obliged to make new burying-grounds, besides that I have mentioned in Bunhill Fields, some of which were continued, and remain in use to this day.[22]

However, almost all of the literature for plague pits was written many years later and no archaeological evidence has been found for their existence as separate entities. It seems certain that all of the sites used for plague burial continued to be used for burials until the mid-nineteenth century.

Liverpool Street Station and Broadgate, EC2 (Bethlem or New Ground)

This site was used during times of plague, and at other times by parishes with limited burial space. It continued in use until around 1720. It originally disappeared under the Broad Street Station booking office (opened 1875) and now mostly lies under the Broadgate Development.

> Although, as has been shown, the greater part of the burden of accommodating the plague dead fell on the parishes, there were two important civic initiatives in this period,

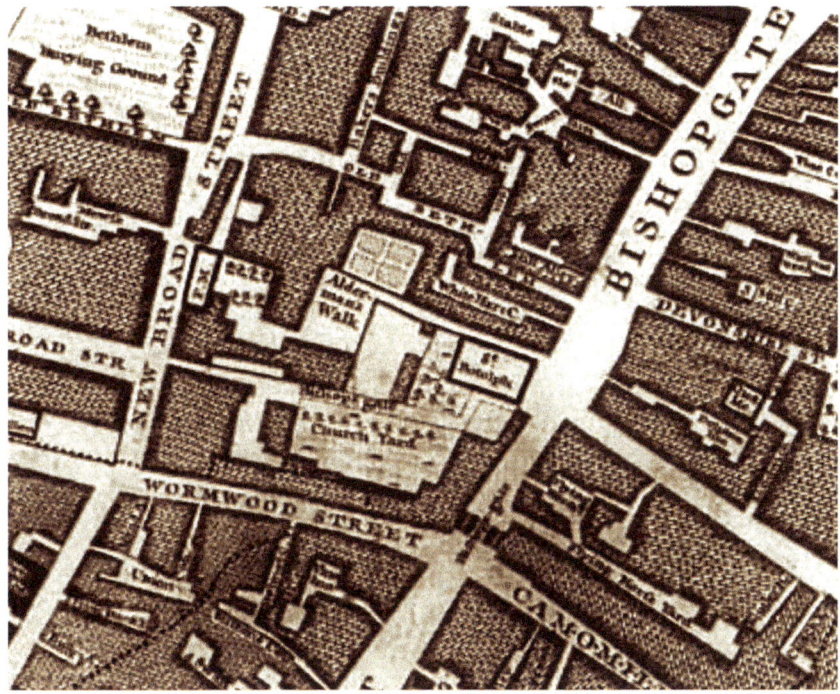

The 1746 Rocque map shows the churchyard on the corner of Wormwood Street and Bishopsgate. The Bethlem Burying Ground to the north-west lies under the Broadgate Development.

---

22 Defoe p.233

which helped to relieve pressure on burial space without resort to irregular burial. The first of these was the creation of the New Churchyard at Bethlem in 1569. Until then London had had no significant extra-parochial burial ground, though St Paul's churchyard in the city centre had always been a popular burial site, especially with inhabitants of the small parishes around the cathedral. Some of the dead in the plague of 1563 were buried there. The high mortality in this epidemic spurred the Mayor and Aldermen to action: in 1569, believing that space in the churchyards of the City might be insufficient if such an epidemic happened again, they decided to establish a new burial ground 'before the time of necessity requireth it'. They chose a site of about one acre already belonging to the City, adjoining the NE side of Moorfields, part of the lands of Bethlem Hospital. The plot, until then used as a tenterground, was walled in, at the expense of Sir Thomas Rowe, then Lord Mayor, usually credited as the New Churchyard's founder. Though the immediate incentive was the fear of an excessive number of plague dead, and the New Churchyard was certainly used for many burials in later epidemics, it was also used extensively in non-plague years by a number of parishes with limited local accommodation, and remained in use to the mid-eighteenth century.[34]

A trench for electrical cables was dug in 2004 between Finsbury Market and Bishopsgate which ran through the western end of Liverpool Street. A large number of bones and two complete skeletons were uncovered that 'almost certainly derive from the "New Cemetery", or "Bethlem Church Ground", which gains its name from the Priory and Hospital of Saint Mary Bethlehem that was historically situated in the vicinity of Liverpool Street. The "New Cemetery", which had previously been a garden, was in use between 1569 and 1720, and was intended to relieve pressure on overcrowded churchyards within the City.'(Site code FWD04. London Archaeologist round up, 2004.)

This ground now largely resides under the Broadgate development and the ground had an interesting history:

> In 1569 Sir Thomas Roe, or Rowe, Merchant Taylor and Mayor, gave about one acre of land in the Moorfields 'for Burial Ease to such parishes in London as wanted convenient ground'. It was especially intended for the parish of St.Botolph's, Bishopsgate, and was probably used for the interment of lunatics from the neighbouring asylum, besides being used by St.Bartholomew's Hospital...the Churchyard and the Asylum have disappeared, Liverpool Street Station having taken their place, and hundreds of the Great Eastern Railway goods vans daily roll over the mouldering remains of the departed citizens.[23]

Part of the site was excavated in 1986. Burials were found to be very dense. A brick vault was found containing members of the Jenks family in lead coffins, dated between 1686

---

23 Holmes, p.176

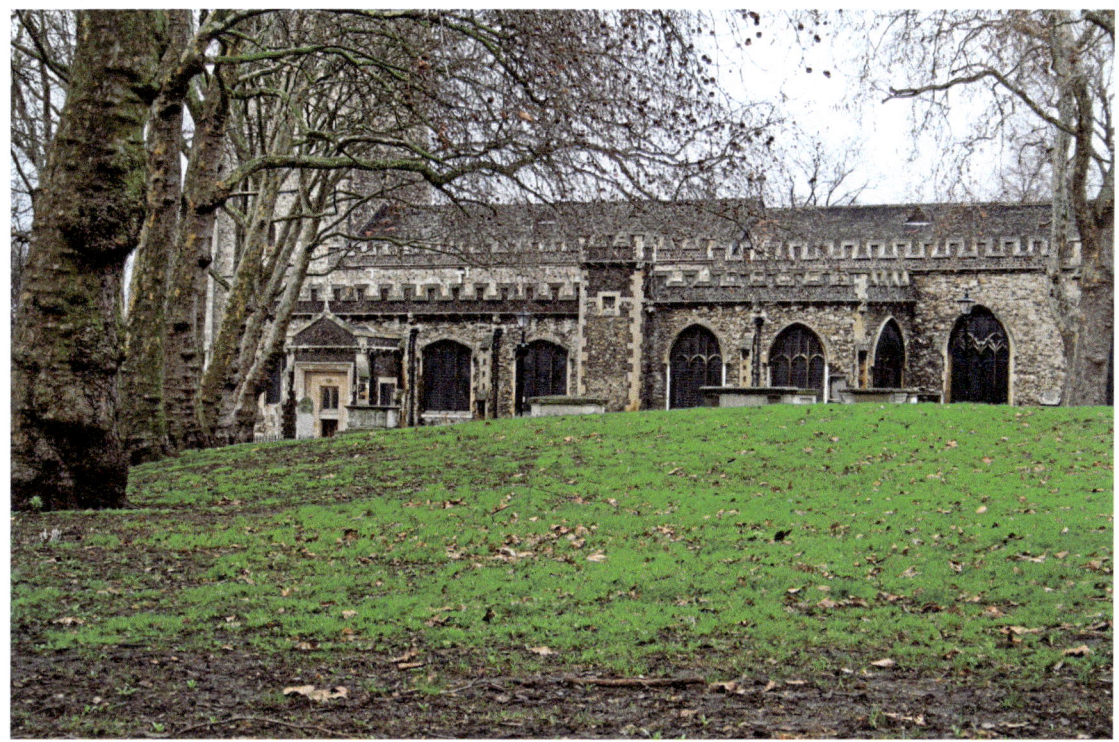

Stepney Churchyard (St Dunstan). The railed-off dog-walking area is the site of the plague pit referred to by Daniel Defoe. In 1886, while laying out this area as a public garden, human remains without coffins were disturbed very near to the surface. (Photograph by R. Bard)

and 1714.[24] Further excavation took place as part of the Crossrail project in 2015 and has uncovered around 3,500 skeletons, including mass burial pits, probably a reaction to a catastrophic event. At the time of writing, analysis of the findings is continuing.

Of the five grounds given by Defoe as plague burial sites for the parish of Stepney, two are the Parish Church of St Paul's in Shadwell and St John in Wapping.

St John's Church, Wapping, Green Bank, E1, (Additional Ground Opposite)

The Church and its environs are worth a visit. The school next to the church has now been converted into private apartments. The vaults of the church were emptied in the 1980s, while the burials in the churchyard were moved to East London Cemetery in 1997. Around 430 individual burials were removed from the site for reburial; of these, 126 could be identified from their coffin plates. The churchyard was divided into three areas: a communal burial vault in the north-east corner of the site containing 41 separate coffins; a series of ten family burial vaults along the

---

24 See David Orme for this information

south boundary wall of the site which held 44 in total; and the remainder of the burial area, containing around 345 individuals. A great many disarticulated remains were also recovered, mainly from a reinterment pit in the centre of the southern area of the site, and from a construction trench around the apse of the church. Approximately 100 burials had been reinterred in the trench, while the large pit contained the remains of over 1,700 individuals, moved during the construction of the docks. (Site code SJN97, London Archaeologist Round-up 1997.) The area of the church and churchyard are atmospheric and retain the feeling of an earlier age. The churchyard is extensive, but the section which is alleged to be the site of the plague pit is the additional ground, the site of the old church, entered by a gate directly opposite the 1760 church entrance. This ground continued in use up until 1854. Holmes describes the churchyard as being 'rather over ½ acre. This was one of the Stepney pest-fields. It is closed but tidy. There are quantities of tombstones in this ground, many of which seem to be falling to pieces, and an unusual number of trees and flowering shrubs.'

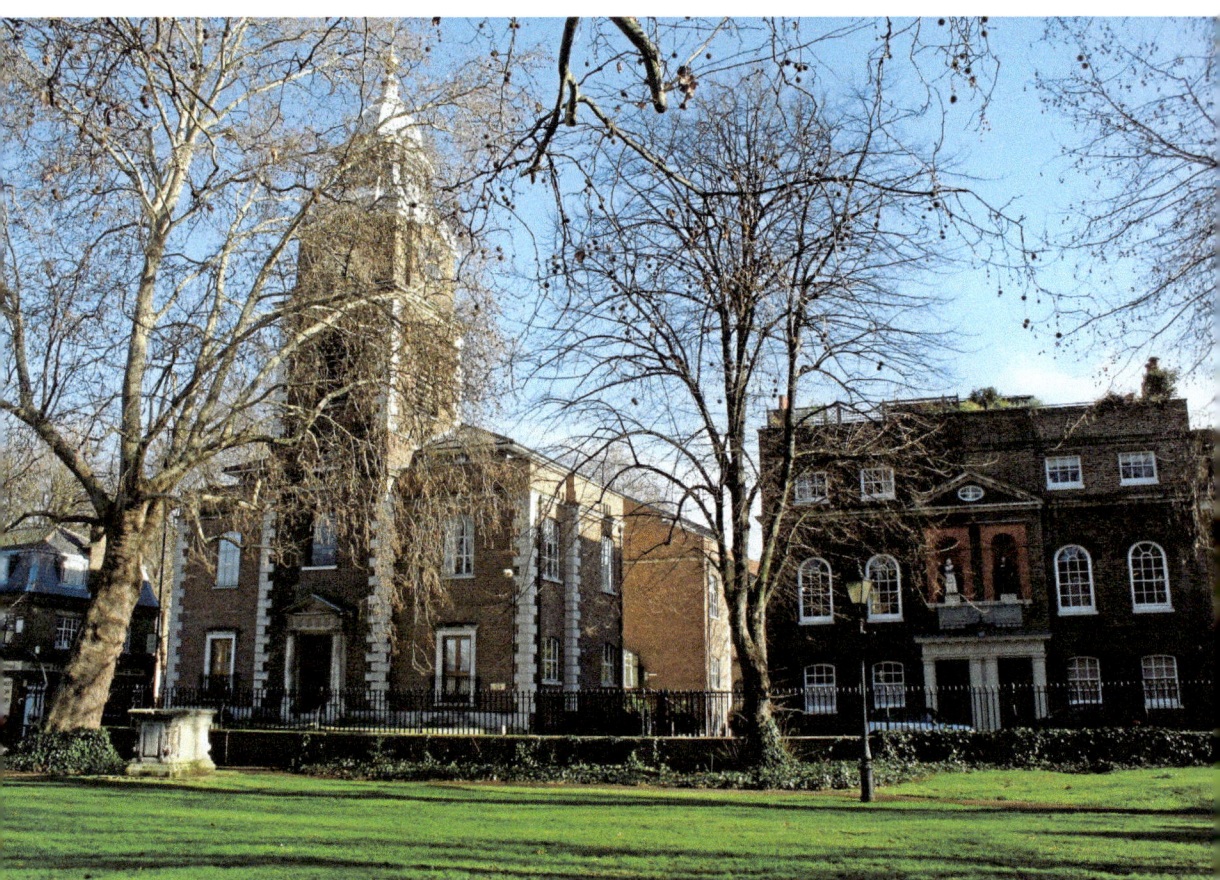

St John's burial ground. The possible site of a 1665 plague pit. The school building on the right was dedicated in 1760, the same date as the church. (Photograph by R. Bard)

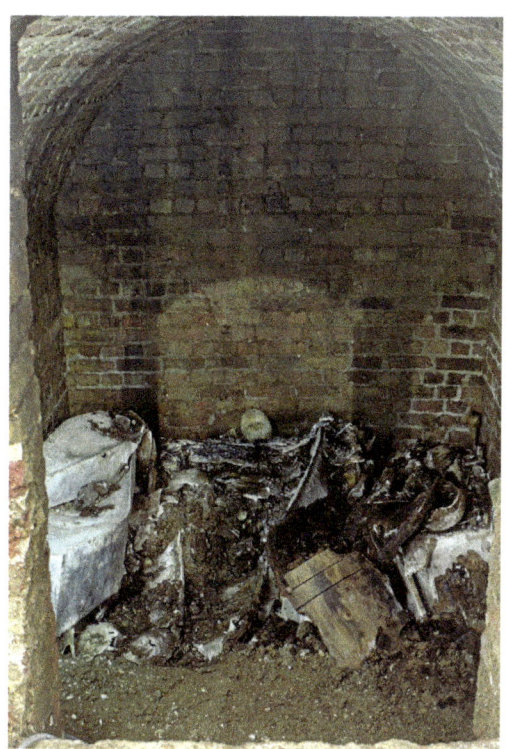

One of ten family faults uncovered between the church and school. See photo above. (A. Miles ©MOLA)

After the two churches, there are three further sites mentioned by Defoe which Holmes looks to identify. She comments that 'one was possibly in Gower's Walk, Whitechapel, where human remains, without coffins were come upon recently [1896] in digging the foundation for Messrs. Kinloch's new buildings. The remains were moved in boxes to a railway arch in Battersea in the winter of 1893–4.'[25] She continues to say that she saw the excavation herself. However, this is likely to have been part of Sheen's Ground, covered later.

Holmes writes '…it is certain that a large tract of land south of the London Hospital was also used for interments, and the Brewer's Garden and the site of St Philip's Church were probably parts of this ground, which was known as Stepney Mount.'[26] The Brewer's Gardens were located a short distance along the street from St Philip's Church.

Holmes describes a large area to the immediate south of the hospital as being a burial ground. She writes that

> the 'unclaimed corpses' from the London Hospital found their last resting-place very near home. In 1849 the whole of the southern part of the enclosure, quite an acre and

---

25 Holmes, p.127
26 Holmes, p.127

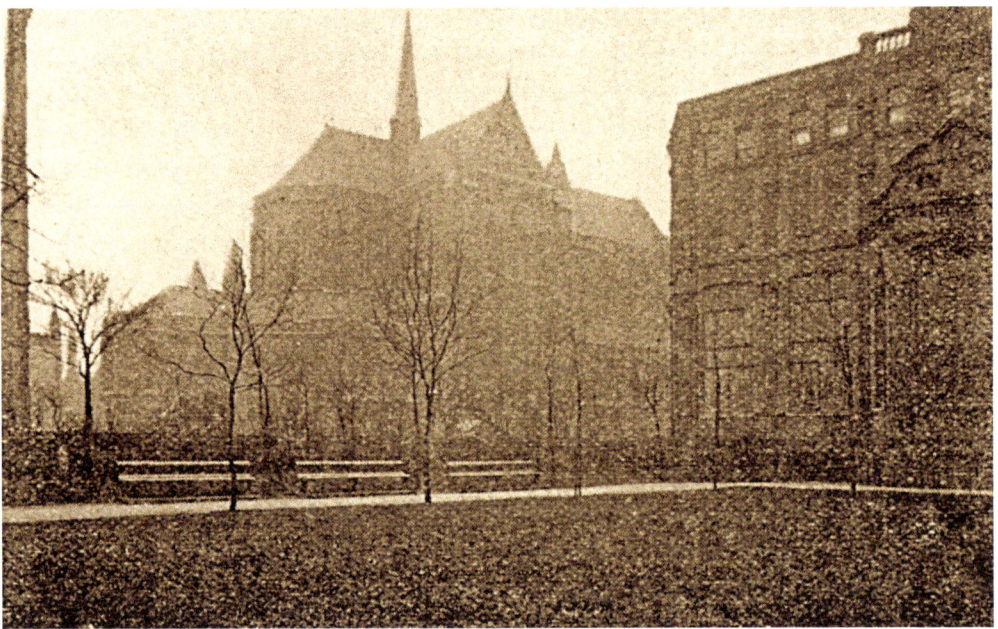

St Philip's Church, adjoining the London Hospital, reputedly covers a 1665 plague pit. (Photograph by R. Bard)

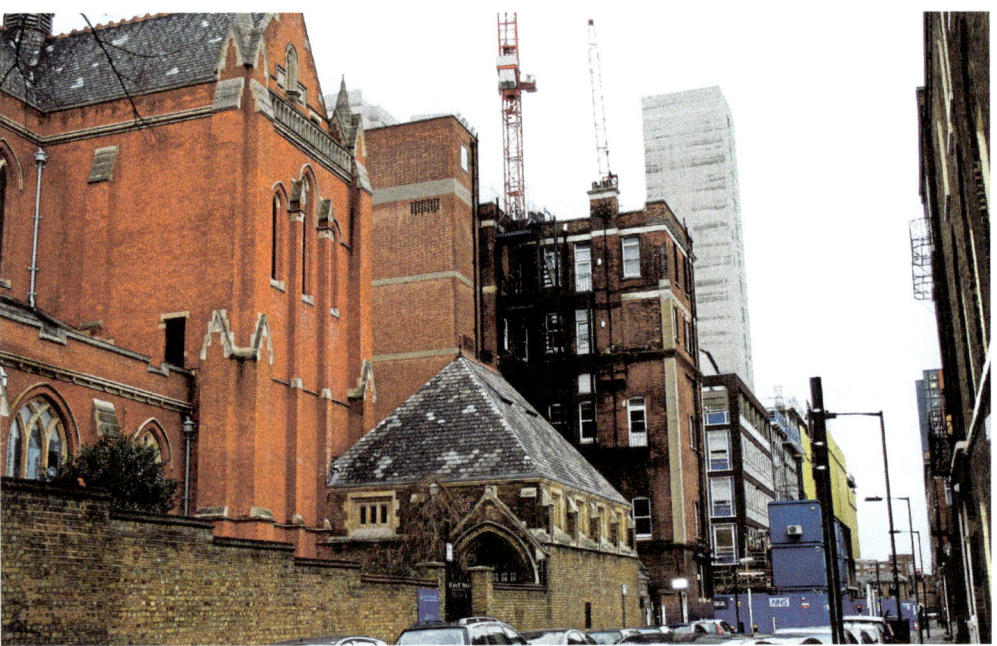

Note the position of the steeple peeping up on the far side of St Philip's Church and the position of the visible section of the London Hospital where the cranes project. Aligning with the 1896 Holmes photograph places much of the foreground of the picture as part of the London Hospital burial ground. (Holmes)

a half, was the burial ground, and here, although it was closed by order in Council in 1854, it appears that burials took place until about 1860, one of the present porters remembering his father acting as a gravedigger. The medical school, the chaplain's house, and the nurse's home have all been built upon it, and it is sincerely to be hoped that no further encroachments will be permitted. The remaining part is the nurse's and student's garden and tennis-court, where they are in the habit of capering about in their short times off duty, and where it sometimes happens that the grass gives way beneath them – an ordinary occurrence when the subsoil is inhabited by coffins!' [27]

In 2006–07 the Museum of London Archaeology carried out excavations in two of the hospital burial grounds during the redevelopment of an area to the south-east of the original hospital building. The remains of 259 people were recovered. Many of these unclaimed patients – mostly adult and male – had been the subject of anatomisation or autopsy, human dissection taking place alongside the vivisection and dissection of dogs, domestic rabbits, horse and cattle as well as exotic species such as the mona monkey, presumably as practice (Fowler and Powers, 2014).

Tothill Fields, Vincent Square, SW1

The area that is now the playing field of Westminster School, Vincent Square, is part of the original Tothill Fields, as it was in the time of Holmes. She describes the area as comprising 8 acres in which 'some buildings have been erected'. She comments that 'A stone-paved yard in Earl Street is said to be the site of the plague pits, now the yard of Her Majesty's Stationary Office, Waste Paper Department.'

This would place the plague pits under Marsham Street, between Horseferry Road and Vincent Street. Earl Street is now that part of Marsham Street, the area where the playing fields are probably contained. There is little to see now except for the playing fields themselves, to which access is restricted.

The 'Five Houses' or 'Seven Chimneys' were built here too, as pesthouses for victims of the plague. In 1665 many of those who had fallen victim to that direful scourge were buried here. Under the date of 18 July 1665, Samuel Pepys writes in his 'Diary': 'I was much troubled this day to hear at Westminster how the officers do bury the dead in the open Tuttle Fields, pretending want of room elsewhere; whereas the New Chapel churchyard was walled in at the publick charge in the last plague-time, merely for want of room, and now none but such as are able to pay dear for it can be buried there.' Here, a short while previously, some '1,200 Scotch prisoners, taken at the battle of Worcester' were interred; for in the accounts of the churchwardens of St Margaret's, Westminster, there is the payment of 'thirty shillings for sixty-seven loads of soil laid on the graves of Tothill Fields, wherein', it is added, 'the Scotch prisoners are buried'. Some of the Scotch were 'driven like a herd of swine', says Heath's 'Chronicle',

---

27 Holmes pp.174-175

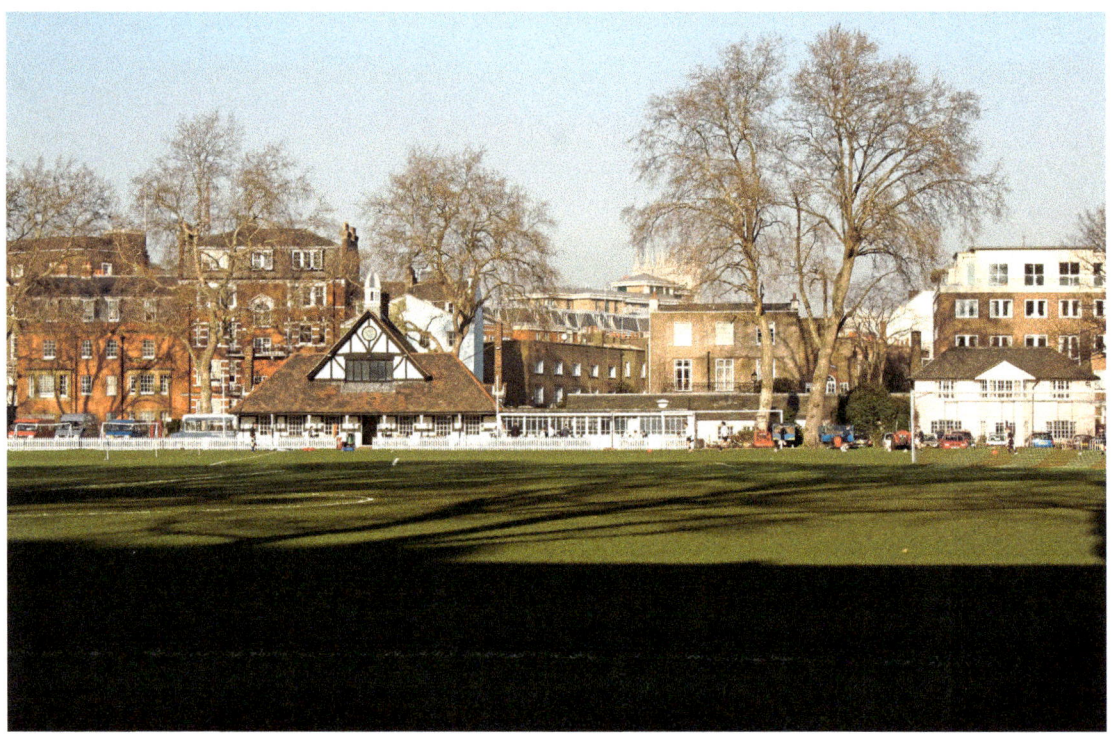

Westminster School Playing Fields. (Photograph by R. Bard)

'through Westminster to Tuthill Fields' and there sold to several merchants, and sent to the island of Barbadoes.

> The 'Five Houses', if we may trust the Builder, retained much of their primitive appearance in 1832. 'With the moss and lichens growing on the roofs and walls, and their generally old-fashioned quaintness, a very small stretch of the imagination removed the buildings which had surrounded them even then, and brought them once more into the open ground. They marked the site of a battery and breastwork when the fortifications around the cities of London and Westminster were hurriedly thrown up in 1642, by an order of Parliament. This battery is marked as about midway between the Chelsea Road and the bank of the river opposite Vauxhall.[28]

Lillie Road Pest Field, Fulham

More distant from the plague burial grounds mentioned by Defoe, is one mentioned by Holmes in 1896, which was in Fulham and referred to as the Lillie Road Pest Field. Holmes writes:

---

28 From: *Westminster: Tothill Fields and Neighbourhood*, Old and New London: Volume 4 (1878), pp. 14-26.

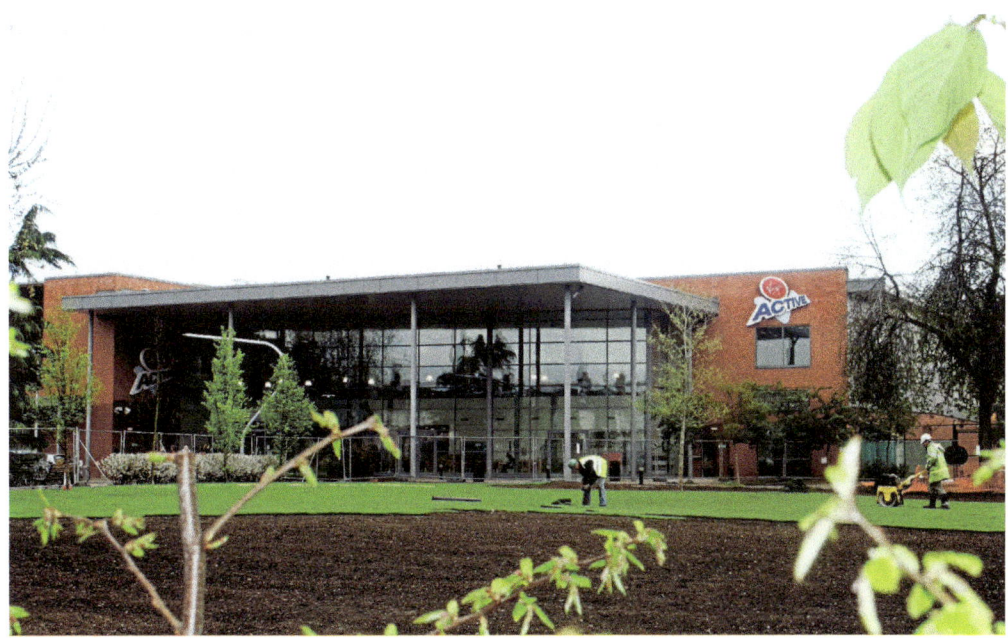

The site of the Fulham Pools. Much of Normand Park is a former plague and pest field burial ground. (Photograph by R. Bard)

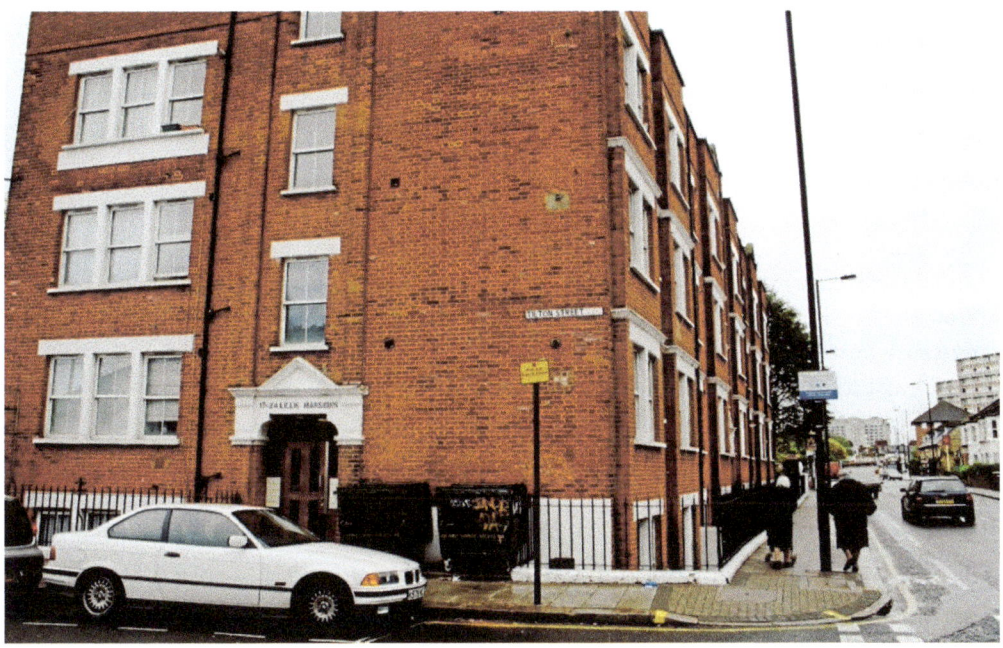

Lillie Road Mansions on the corner of Tilton Street. Lillie Road Pest Field (at one time the orchard of Normand House) 'was used extensively for burials at the time of the Great Plague. Only about ¾ of an acre is still unbuilt upon, at the corner of Tilton Street, and this is offered for sale.' (Holmes, 1896) (Photograph by R. Bard)

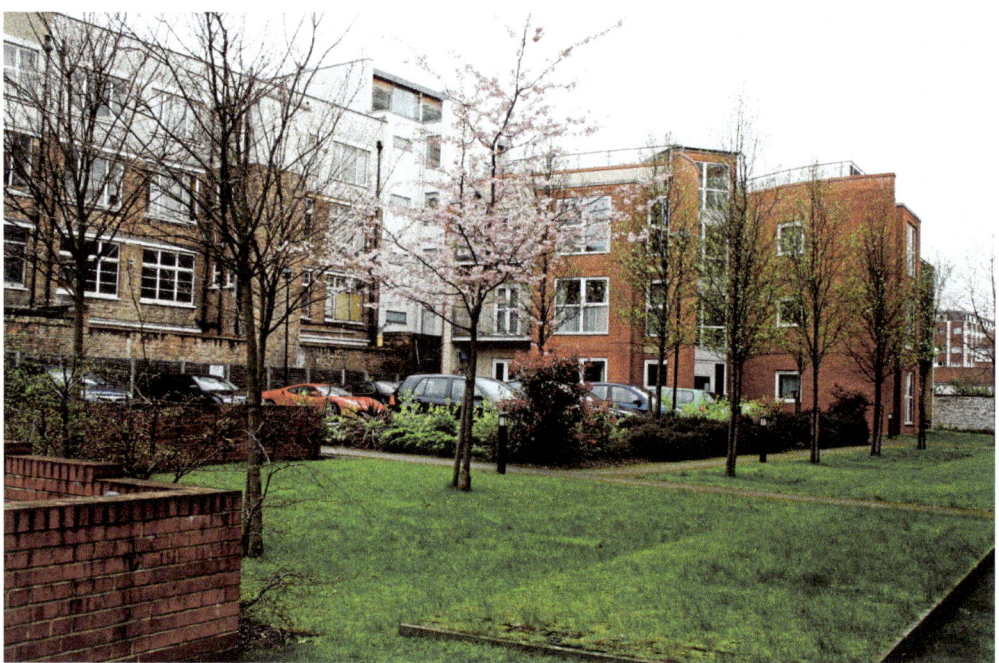

Mount Mills area of Defoe's plague pit from 1665. (Photograph by R. Bard)

> Lillie Road Pest Field (the orchard of Normand House).—The site of this orchard, then 4 acres in extent, was used extensively for burials at the time of the Great Plague, Lintaine Grove now occupies part of it, and a row of houses in Lillie Road. Only about ¾ of an acre is still unbuilt upon, at the corner of Tilton Street, and this is offered for sale.[29]

The site of the former pest field and plague burial ground is now being developed as Normand Park. Normand Park now covers much of the site, and Fulham Pools swimming baths now covers a section of the site as well. The ¾ of an acre of unbuilt land that Holmes commented on in 1896 on the corner of Lillie Road and Tilton Street is now Lillie Road Mansions.

The Mount Mill area, which sits slightly back from Goswell Street is a narrow, atmospheric residential street, which, according to Defoe, also hosts a lost burial ground, barely 300 yards away from Seward Street itself. The area of the plague pit is partly in the car park and partly in the residential garden.

Maitland in his *Survey of London*, 1739, comments that,

> Part of Bunhill Fields, at present denominated Tindal's, or the Dissenters' great Burial Ground, was, by the Mayor and Citizens of London, in the year 1665, set apart and

---

29 Holmes p.282

consecrated as a common cemetery, for the interment of such corpses as could not have room in their own parochial burial-grounds in that dreadful year of pestilence. However, it not being made use of on that occasion, the said Tindal took a lease thereof, and converted it into a burial-ground for the use of Dissenters.[30]

Two earlier sources, Strype in 1720 and Defoe in 1722, state otherwise, and it seems unlikely that at a time where burial land was in such urgent need that it wouldn't have been used for this purpose. As Vanessa Harding says,

> It seems highly improbable that a ground created specifically for plague burial and presumably available for use by October at the latest, when weekly deaths were still running at over 4,000, would not have been used extensively. Indeed the City's order, on the same day as the commission to Robinson, that the keeper of the New Churchyard should desist from making pits there and dig only single graves (and its later comment that he had done so) implies that alternative space was quickly made available. References in some parish registers to burials in 'the new ground' from September 1665 could be to Bunhill Fields, though they might also be to new parochial grounds.[31]

St James Workhouse Burial Ground, Poland Street/Carnaby Street, W1 and Golden Square, W1 (Originally Pawlett's Gardens)

The site of this former burial ground lies in the heart of tourist London, a few hundred yards from Carnaby Street and Regent Street. The Marshall Street burial grounds were part of the additional graveyards that were developed by the parish of St James, Westminster, in the seventeenth and eighteenth centuries. As Soho grew, from largely agricultural land to a built-up area from the mid-seventeenth century, and as the population increased, so did the pressure mount on burial space in the parish churchyard on Piccadilly. The response of the parish is seen in the Lower Ground, which opened in 1694 when the land was obtain from Lord Craven; the Upper Ground, which opened in 1735; and the new workhouse complex, which was constructed between 1725–27.

> The burial ground was in use as an overflow from St James, Piccadilly, from 1693. The St.James's workhouse was built in 1728 partly over the burial ground. At a vestry meeting it was computed that the new ground would hold 12,000 bodies, 'which rot so fast that 800 may annually be buried in it.' In 1711 the vestry received a complaint about the smoke issuing from the chimney of Cope the grave- makers house in the burial ground. The smoke was noisome and offensive; and was caused by the Burning of Old Rotten Coffin Boards, and by his Wife Frequent Laundering for People; By 1733 the ground was in use until the

---

30 Quoted from Wade, p.45.
31 Vanessa Harding, http://www.history.ac.uk/cmh/epiharding.html

purchase of a new plot of land for use for burial on Hampstead Road in 1789. The workhouse burial ground was attached to the parish ground, but was kept separate, remaining in use until 1793, when the parish started using Hampstead Road for all its extramural burials. Holmes tells us in her time a work-house was built upon a common cemetery where, at the time of the plague, many thousands of bodies were interred. A small part of it was kept as the workhouse burial-ground, but this has now disappeared, and all that is left of the original ground used for interments is the garden or courtyard of the workhouse. Holmes writes, 'It is a pleasant recreation ground for the inmates, and is well supplied with seats, being about ¼ acre in extent.' (p.285).

A later burial ground was associated with the workhouse and its chapel to the south until it closed, and the area was covered by the public baths built in 1851. Part of the original church's burial area was retained as a central courtyard to the workhouse. The workhouse was finally closed in 1913, and the building was used to house refugees during the Second World War. After the war, the building lay empty until 1925 when the site was redeveloped.

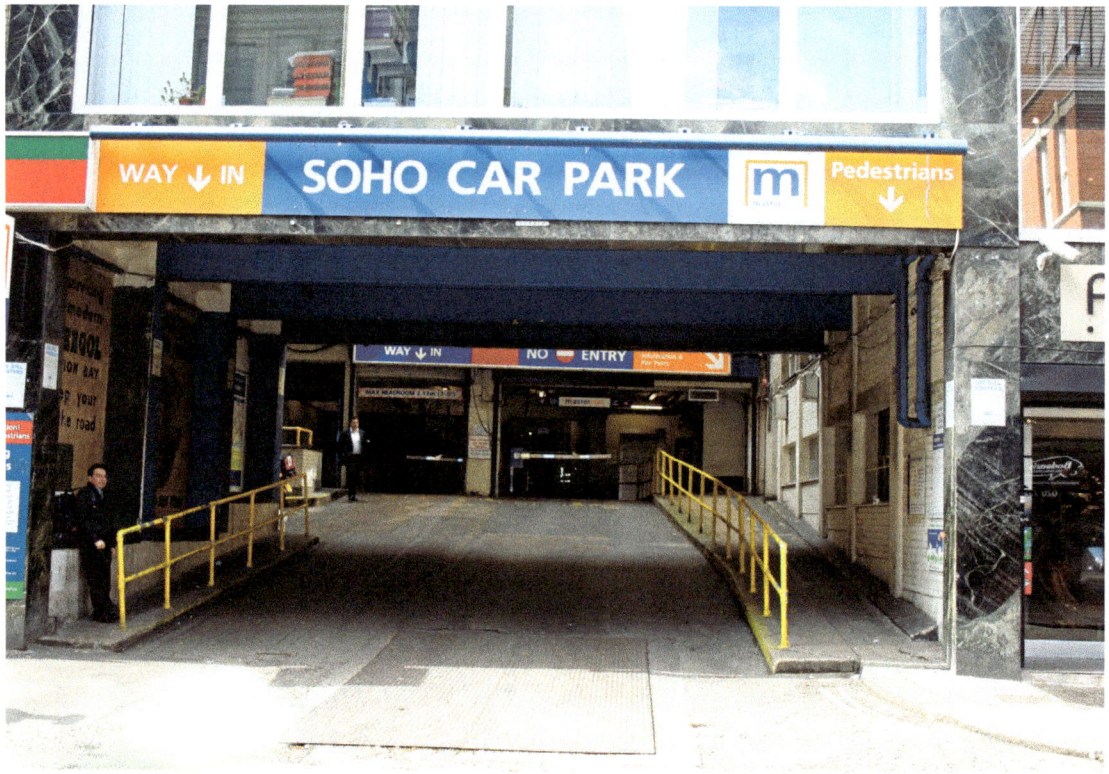

The Soho Car, Poland Street, from D'Arblay Street, which was, in the eighteenth century, Portland Street (*see* Rocque map). The burial grounds lie partly under the garage and extends back as far as Marshall Street. (Photograph by R. Bard)

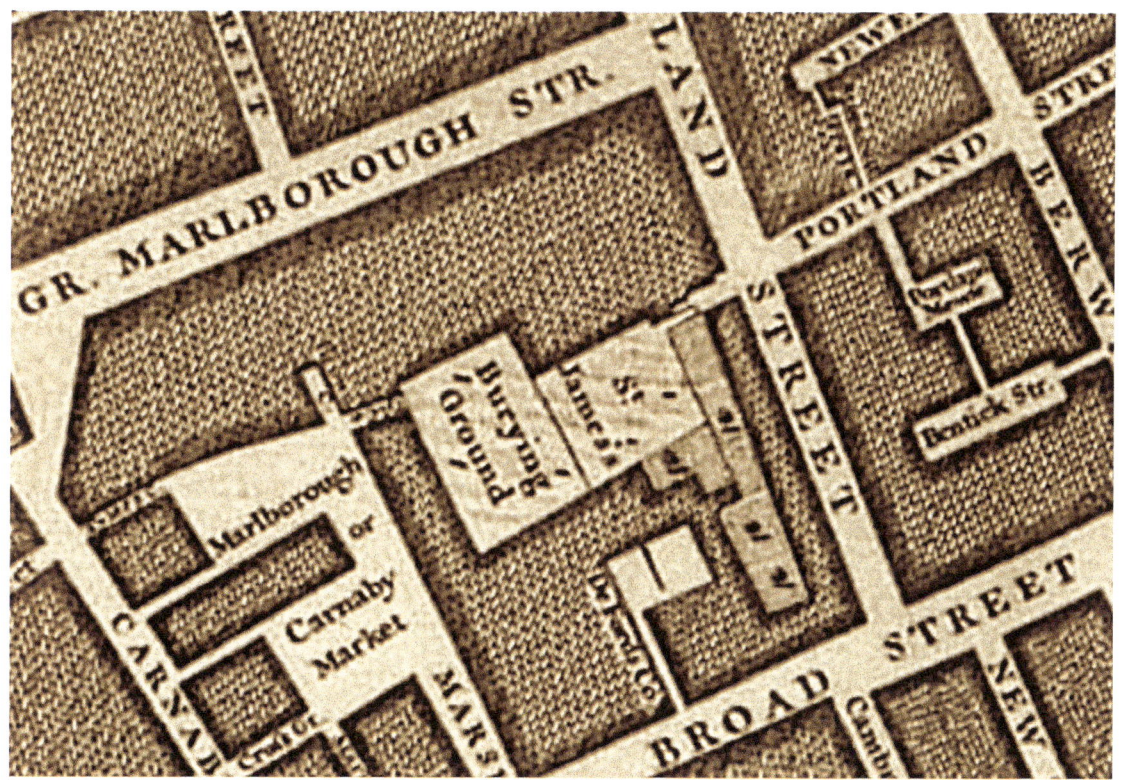

The Rocque map of 1746 showing the St James's Burying Ground situated on the corner opposite the present-day Fouberts Place and Marshall Street. Broad Street is now Broadwick Street.

The area of Portland Street leading to the eastern side of the burial ground is now Dufour's Place, which was Pesthouse Close until the early eighteenth century. The Marshall Street Baths, which have been renovated and reopened in 2010, sits on the southern end of the extension to the parish ground. As part of the renovations of the baths and the conversion of the adjacent car park into flats in 2008–09, archaeological excavations were carried out, during which 2,550 burials were recorded from parts of all three burial grounds. This represents only a small percentage, with many still surviving under the existing buildings.

Infected persons were isolated in pesthouses, and often, in the immediate vicinity, were buried in 'Pest Fields'. The 1878 London History *Old and New London* reports such a pest field existed in the heart of London's West End. Carnaby Street was the site of a pesthouse, and thousands were buried in the immediate vicinity:

> Golden Square and Wardour Street now form the western and eastern limits. The property in this vicinity of old belonged to Lord Craven, who erected the famous pest-house here for the reception of those struck by the plague. The historian Maitland, in his 'History of London' mentions the Pest Field: The site whereon

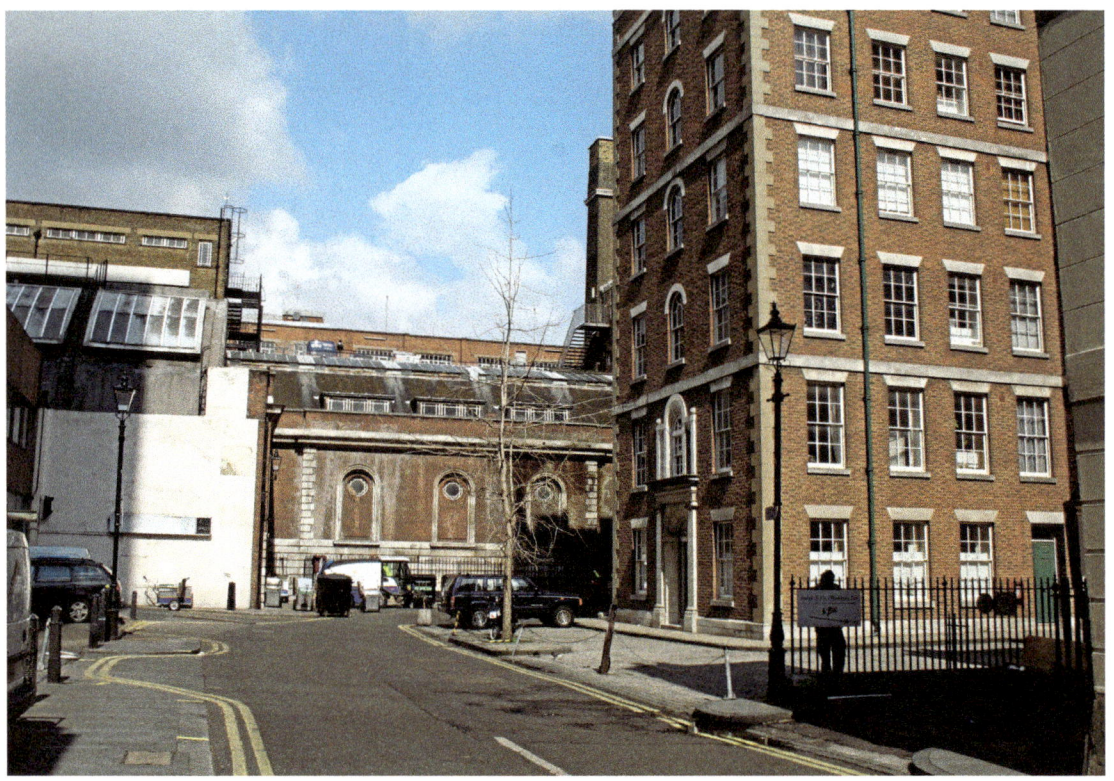

Dufour's Place, formerly part of Pesthouse Close. The building in the centre rear is the Marshall Street Baths, now reopened. It is situated on part of the extension to the burial ground. (Photograph by R. Bard)

Marshall Street, part of Little Broad Street, and Marlborough Market are now erected, was denominated the Pest Field, from a lazaretto therein, which consisted of thirty-six small houses, for the reception of poor and miserable objects of this neighbourhood that were afflicted with the direful pestilence of 1665. And at the lower end of Marshall Street, contiguous to Silver Street, was a common cemetery, wherein some thousands of corpses were buried that died of that dreadful and virulent contagion.... When Carnaby Street and other streets were built, a field on the Paddington estate was assigned as a pest-field in place of that which we have described.

3. London's Worst Nineteenth-Century Burial Grounds

As mentioned in the introduction, the continued burial of the many thousands of Londoners that died annually in the overcrowded churchyards of inner London led to not only appalling sanitary conditions and premature deaths, but an agitation to reform the laws that allowed inner-city burials. Burial grounds had been abused by private owners eager for profit, which led to burial pit interments for many of the poor, and the almost immediate reuse of graves. It was not uncommon for the mourners to be ushered away from the newly used graveside, without the gravedigger having filled it in with earth. The body would be removed to a waiting pit, usually in a disused, or at least inconspicuous, corner of the churchyard. Those burials that took place were often several bodies deep, and it was not unusual for the top burial to be inches from the surface, or in some cases to protrude through. Some of London's best-known tourist sites, such as St Margaret Parish Church adjoining Westminster Abbey, St Martin-in-the-Fields, and St Ann's in Soho, were only a few examples of grounds where unhygienic and offensive sights were ever-present. In some of these graveyards it was not uncommon for bones and bits of coffins to be scattered for all to see. Walker reported to Parliament and named a number of grounds that were causing offence and were unhygienic. The Chadwick Report, published in 1842, portrayed a bleak picture:

> In the metropolis, on spaces of ground which do not exceed 203 acres, closely surrounded by the abodes of the living, layer upon layer, each consisting of a population numerically equivalent to a large army of 20,000 adults, and nearly 30,000 youths and children, is every year imperfectly interred. Within the period of the existence of the present generation, upwards of a million of dead must have been interred in those same spaces.

He continues by painting a graphic picture of the consequences of so many 'imperfectly interred' corpses:

> A layer of bodies is stated to be about seven years in decaying in the metropolis: to the extent that this is so, the decay must be by the conversion of the remains into gas, and its escape, as a miasma, of many times the bulk of the body that has disappeared.

This conclusion was undoubtedly reached by the proliferation of reports of the time that gravediggers sometimes perished on the spot from inhaling such gases. In some of the populous parishes, where, from the nature of the soil, the decomposition has not been so rapid as the interments, the place of burial has risen in height; and the height of many of them must have greatly increased but for the surreptitious modes of diminishing it by removal, which, it must be confessed, has diminished the sanitary evil, though by the creation of another and most serious evil, in the mental pain and apprehensions of the survivors and feelings of abhorrence of the population, caused by the suspicion and knowledge of the disrespect and desecration of the remains of the persons interred.[32]

Reformers looked abroad to see how matters were handled in France and Germany in particular, and came to the conclusion that city burials needed to be banned. Walker's report, along with the first appearance of Dickens's *Bleak House* resulted in the Metropolitan Interments Act of 1850. It is worth a detailed look at some of the Walker sites – many of which still exist, and some lie under modern buildings and car parks. From the relatively sanitary conditions of modern London, many of these sites, when visited with the knowledge of what went before, can be very poignant and atmospheric.

The Additional Ground in Drury Lane (Now Drury Lane Gardens), Drury Lane, WC2

This ground, which was an additional ground to St Martins-in-the-Fields, is situated in the heart of theatre land and is found armed with the Dickensian descriptions of its previous incarnation making this 'garden', which is now mostly a children's playground, extremely atmospheric. As one enters the ground from Drury Lane, on the right is the old watch house and mortuary building. Against the right-hand wall discretely rest half a dozen extremely worn tombstones. Buildings of a much later vintage than Dickens still surround the burial ground, and there is a brief history near the entrance. It was once one of the most appalling grounds in London. Dickens wrote a letter from Boston in 1868 to a Miss Palfrey describing the ground when he was a child:

Letter to Miss Palfrey, 4th April 1868.

Convey yourself back to London by the agency of that powerful locomotive, your imagination, and walk through the centre avenue of Covent Garden market from West to East: – that is to say, with your back towards the church, and your face towards Drury Lane Theatre. Keep straight on along the side of the theatre, and about half way down, on the left side of the way, behind the houses, is a closely hemmed-in grave yard - happily long disused and closed by the law. I do not remember that the

---

32 Chadwick Report, p.27

graveyard is accessible from the street now, but when I was a boy it was to be got at by a low covered passage under a house, and was guarded by a rusty iron gate. In that churchyard I long afterwards buried the 'Nemo' of Bleak House.[33]

George Walker describes this ground in 1839 as follows:

many thousands of bodies have been here deposited. The substratum was, some years since, so saturated with dead, that the place 'was shut up' for a period. The ground was subsequently raised to its present height – *level with the first floor windows surrounding the place,* and in this super stratum vast numbers of bodies have, up to this period, been deposited. A short time since a pit was dug (a very common practice here) in one corner of the ground; in it many bodies were deposited at different periods, the top of the pit being covered only with boards. This ground is a most intolerable and highly dangerous nuisance to the entire neighbourhood. Rather more than two years ago, in making three areas to the centre houses on the western side of the burying ground, many bodies were disturbed and mutilated; the inhabitants of the houses are frequently annoyed by the most disgusting and repulsive sights.[34]

Holmes describes the ground in 1896 as a well-kept public garden of less than ¼ acre: 'It is well kept, and contains some gymnastic apparatus for the use of the children. Also called the Tavistock burial-ground.'

Walker describes the ground, which belonged to St Mary le Strand, as being a health hazard:

in its original state it was below the level of the adjoining ground, - now, the surface is on a line with the first floor windows of the houses entirely surrounding this place. It has long been in a very disgusting condition, but within the last month the surface has been "cleaned up," and the whole may now be called "the whited sepulchre." A man who had committed suicide was buried here on the 20th May, 1832; the body was in the most offensive condition, and was placed within a very little distance of the surface. About twenty years ago, Mr. -----, a very respectable tradesman in the neighbourhood, was employed to make a" cold air drain" at the west end of this ground; for this purpose it was necessary to cut through the wall of an adjoining house; on taking up the ground floor of this house, large quantities of human bones were found scattered about, - it was supposed they had been dragged thither by rats, vast numbers of which annoy the inhabitants in the proximity of this burying ground.[35]

---

33 Dickens, letter written from Boston dated 4 April 1868. I am grateful to David Orme for bringing this letter to my attention.
34 Walker, p.162,163
35 Walker, pp 163-164

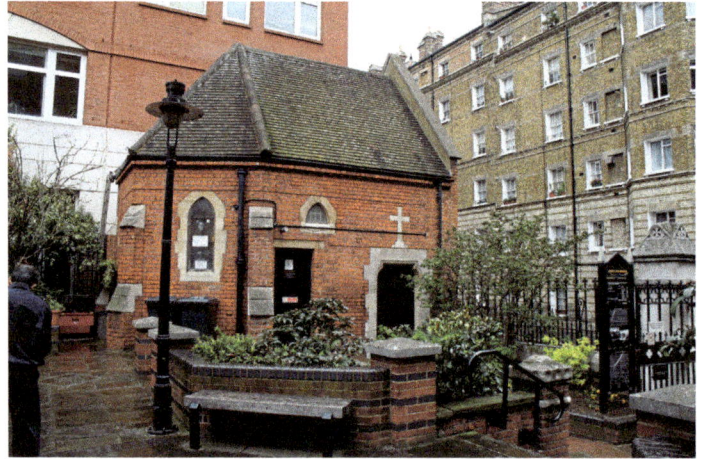

The old mortuary building where bodies were kept prior to burial, looking towards the now main entrance to the gardens in Drury Lane. (Photograph by R. Bard)

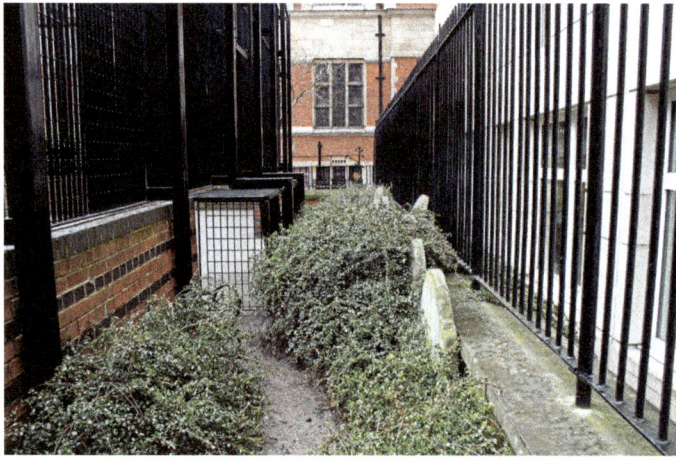

The only visible reminders of what lie underneath this children's playground. (Photograph by R. Bard)

By 1897, when Holmes described it, there was little to associate it with Walker's 1839 description:

> 430 square yards. It is probable that few grounds in London were more overcrowded with bodies than this one, which was entirely surrounded by the backs of small houses. When closed in 1853 it was in a very disgusting and unwholesome condition, and it continued to be most wretched until the Metropolitan Public Gardens Association asphalted it in 1886. It is maintained as a children's playground by the London County Council. This is the scene of 'Tom all Alone's' in 'Bleak House.' There are 6 gravestones against the wall.

Whitechapel Church (now the Altab Ali Park), Whitechapel Road, E1

There is now little to see unless one knows where to look. The site itself has now been renamed the Altab Ali Park. On entry there are a few tombs scattered around, mostly as you come in, but otherwise the ground has been completely levelled. There is a white-chalk outline ingrained into the grass to show where the last church once stood. This churchyard was one of the most overcrowded offenders of the early nineteenth century, as was its now even more hidden and melancholic additional grounds, which still remain as a plot of land behind some houses on the north side of Whitechapel Road.

The earliest known record of the church dates back to 1329. The ground is probably best known for containing the mortal remains of Richard Brandon. Recorded in the parish register in 1649: 'Buriall, June 21, Rich. Brandon, a man out of Rosemary Lane', now Royal Mint Street, and in the margin was added, 'this R Brandon is supposed to have cut off the Head of Charles I'. The execution of Charles I in 1649 was unpopular and the scene at what is now the Altab Ali Park, the site of St Mary's, Whitechapel, can be imagined when Brandon came to be buried. A contemporary document says,

> For the burial whereof, great store of wines were sent by the sheriff of the city of London, and a great multitude of people stood wayting to see his corpse carried to the churchyard, some crying out, 'Hang him, rogue!' 'Bury him in the dunghill!' others pressing upon him, saying they would quarter him for executing the King, insomuch that the churchwardens and masters of the parish were fain to come for the suppression of them; and with great difficulty he was at last carried to Whitechapel churchyard.[36]

On the night of 29 December 1940, the Whitechapel Church was destroyed when it was gutted by fire during an enemy incendiary raid, and the church was demolished in 1952. In 1966 the site of the church and the churchyard was made into a public garden.

Walker has much to say about Whitechapel Church and its adjoining burial ground, including a comment that the vaults under the church were dilapidated, and the smells coming from there were offensive. His main target of attack was the state of the burial ground that adjoined the church, sitting alongside 'one of the greatest thoroughfares in London, and placed in the centre of a densely populated neighbourhood.'[37] He continues, suggesting that the decomposition in this overcrowded burial ground was the cause of much disease 'by which the lower order of the inhabitants of this parish have so frequently been visited.' His report makes grim reading, especially when contrasted to the peaceful gardens that now mark the site:

> The ground is so densely crowded as to present one entire mass of human bones and putrefaction....It appears almost impossible to dig a grave in this ground without coming into contact with some recent interment, and the grave digger's pick is often forced through the lid of a coffin when least expected ... most of the graves are very shallow, -- some entire coffins, indeed, are to be found within a foot and a half of the surface.[38]

---

36 Walker p.168, quoted from Timbs, J. (1855). Curiosities of London: exhibiting the most rare and remarkable objects of interest in the Metropolis, London. P.146,
37 Walker pp.168-169
38 Walker p.168-169

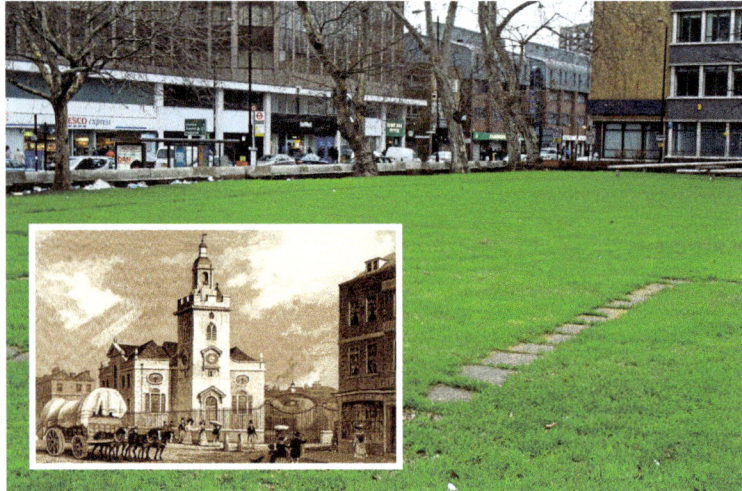

Inset: the original St Mary's Church replaced by a larger building destroyed by fire in 1880.

'... The ground is so densely crowded as to present one entire mass of human bones and putrefaction...' (Walker) (Photograph by R. Bard)

The cavalier attitude to the dead and their remains is one of Walker's primary complaints:

> In digging a foundation for a new wall, on the eastern side of the church, the workmen penetrated through a mass of human bones eight or ten feet in thickness; these bones were thrown out, and for some time lay exposed to public view, scattered over the ground in a loathsome humid state; two or three pits were afterwards dug to the depth of eight or ten feet, as common repositories for these bones; and the pits were filled up to within a few inches of the top, with a slight covering of earth over them; family graves also were disturbed, and many coffins exposed, --some of them literally cut in two; in consequence of which much altercation arose between the churchwardens and parishioners. Coffin wood is plentifully strewed over the ground in a rotten and decomposed state...The *poor ground*, a little distance from the church, is as thickly crowded with the remains of the dead as the burying ground adjoining to the church.[39]

The additional burial ground for St Mary's lay a short distance to the north-east of the church, and was as equally badly overcrowded as the main burial ground.

St Mary's Additional Ground, Whitechapel Road, E1
This burial ground is anonymous and very atmospheric. It is situated almost opposite the site of St Mary's behind the row of shops and offices in Whitechapel Road. To find this ground is not easy. Access is via a cul-de-sac on the Whitechapel Road side of Old Montague Street. The area is slightly rundown and surrounded by houses. The ground undulates ominously.

---

39 Walker p.168-169

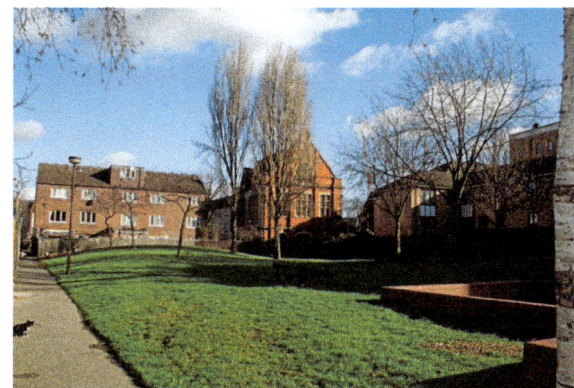

This burial ground at the beginning of the nineteenth century was described as being 'thickly crowded with the remains of the dead'. (Walker, 1839) (Photograph by R. Bard)

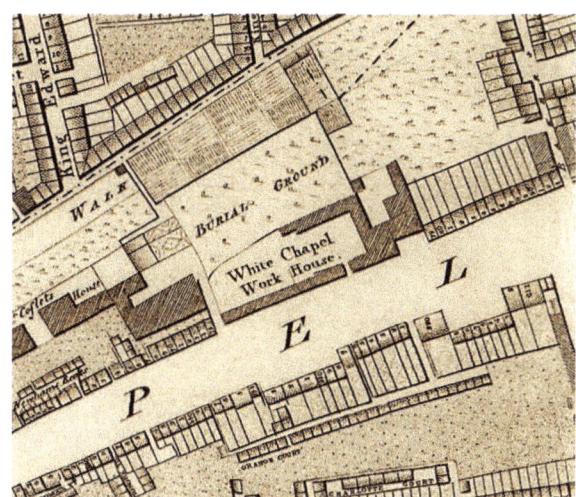

The burial ground as shown in Horwood's 1799 map.

Walker tell us of this burial ground that 'the poor ground, a little distance from the church, is as thickly crowded with the remains of the dead as the burying ground adjoining to the church'.[40]

Holmes tells us that this green piece of ground was the workhouse burial ground:

> the workhouse having been built in 1768 upon a former graveyard, and this piece to the north of it having then been set aside for interments and consecrated in 1796. The workhouse site was built upon some years ago, and the burial-ground became the playground of the Davenant Schools, one of which, the one facing St. Mary's Street, was built in it; in the order for closing it, dated May 9, 1853, it is called the Whitechapel Workhouse and Schools Ground. It is difficult to say exactly how far east the burial-ground extended, but from the Ordnance map and some older plans

---

40 Walker p.169

it would appear that the recent addition to the school in Whitechapel Road has been built in the burial-ground. In 1833 the size was given as 2,776 square yards, but it was stated that in 1832 196 cholera cases were interred in an adjoining piece of ground. This is probably what is now used as a stone-yard, with carts in it.[41]

Interestingly, the adjacent Davenant Centre, which had been the addition to the school in Whitechapel Road mentioned in Holmes, was in 2005 the subject of a Museum of London Archaeology watching brief when, during the refurbishment of the building, sixty burials were found within six small trenches. This confirmed that, as Holmes suspected, the ground had extended further east. (Site code WRA05, London Archaeologist Round-up 2005.)

Burying Ground, (on LSE campus), Portugal Street, Aldwych, WC2

This site was originally, and under the circumstances strangely, known as the 'Green Ground'. It was one of London's most notorious burial grounds. The former site of this ground lies less than a minutes' walk to the north of St Clement Dane Church in the Strand and is mostly situated under and immediately around what is now the site of the London School of Economics' library. George Walker describes the area in 1839:

> This is a narrow thoroughfare on the eastern side of Clare Market; it extends from Clare Market to the Strand, and is surrounded by places, from which they are continually given off emanations from animal putrescence. The back windows of the houses on the east side of the lane look into a burying ground called the 'Green Ground,' in Portugal Street...on the west side the windows (if open) permit the odour of another burying place – a private one, called Enon Chapel – to perflate the houses; at the bottom –the south end—of this Lane, is another burying place, belonging to the Alms Houses (This place is, I believe, filled with dead; many of the coffins being near the surface) within a few feet of the Strand, and in the centre of the Strand are the burying ground and vaults of St. Clement Danes; in addition to which, there are several slaughter houses in the immediate neighbourhood: so that in a distance of about two hundred yards in a direct line there are four burying grounds; and the living here breathe on all sides an atmosphere impregnated with the odour of the dead. The inhabitants of this narrow thoroughfare are very unhealthy; nearly every room in every house is occupied by a separate family. Typhus fever in its aggravated form has attacked by far the majority of the residents, and death has made among them the most destructive ravages.[42]

Portugal Street still remains in the immediate vicinity of the Royal College of Surgeons off the Kingsway just south of Lincolns Inn Fields. The burial ground, which belonged to St Clement Danes, had been a 'burying place beyond the memory of man'.

---

41 Holmes p.296
42 Walker p.149-150

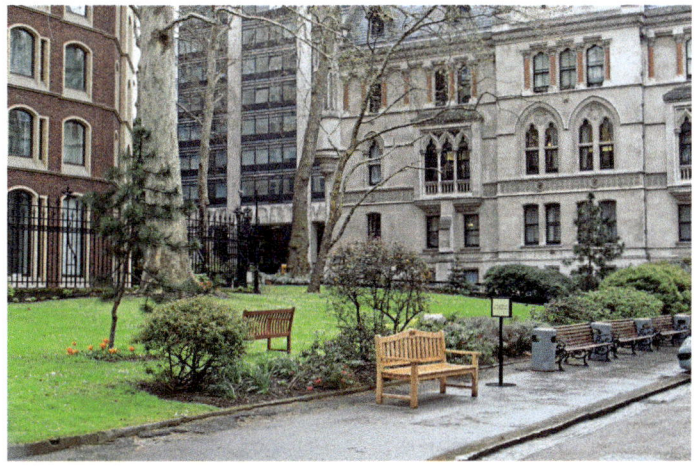

The Alms Houses Burying Ground. The Royal Courts of Justice lie immediately to the right. Walker, 1839, said of this now tranquil piece of ground, 'this place is, I believe, filled with dead; many of the coffins being near the surface'. (Photograph by R. Bard)

> On the south side of Portugal Street, near the centre of the few small courts that have not been swept away, stands King's College Hospital, (founded 1839)...It stands on the site of the old workhouse of St. Clement Danes, and of one of the burial-grounds already mentioned...A part of the buildings of this hospital stands on ground which, up to about the year 1850, was one of the burial-places belonging to the parish. It was about the third of an acre in extent, and called the 'Green Ground,' as if in mockery. From a report of a parochial committee in 1848, we learn that upwards of 5,500 bodies had been interred within it in the previous quarter of a century. The scenes witnessed here were of the most offensive character.[43]

Walker is scathing on the state of the ground and events which took place there. He says,

> The soil of this ground is saturated, absolutely saturated, with human putrescence. On Saturday the 27 April, 1839, at 5, p.m. I went, accompanied by a friend to Nos 30 and 31, Clements Lane, and upon looking through the windows of the back attics, we saw two graves open, close to the south-eastern extremity of this burying ground. Several bones were lying on the surface of the grave nearest to us – a large piece of coffin wood was placed in readiness for removal, and, at a small distance, a heap covered with course sacking, was observed, which, when the covering was taken off, proved also to be long pieces of coffin wood, evidently not in a decayed state. The nails were very conspicuous... The grave diggers were seen to take off tin plates from the coffins broken up...[44]

The breaking up of coffins and desecration of graves were common in the name of profit. It was acceptable practice to allow burials to remain for several years until

---

43 *St Clement Danes: The parish*, Old and New London: Volume 3 (1878), pp. 26-32. Walker, p.150
44 Quoted from Walker, p.151

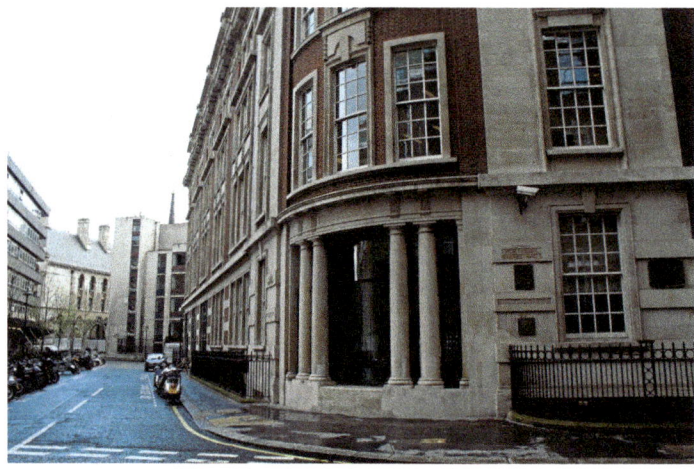

The site of the Portugal Street burial ground on the corner of Carey Street and Portugal Street. One of London's most appalling burial grounds lies under the LSE building. (Photograph by R. Bard)

they decomposed, and then have the bones moved to a charnel house, thus providing extra space in the tightly packed London churchyards. The 'recycling' of these graves allowed for receipt of extra burial fees, and bribes to sextants, at the expense of hygiene and dignity. Walker quotes a letter to the *Times* dated 25 June 1838:

> Sir, passing along Portugal Street on Saturday evening, about ten minutes before seven, I was much shocked at seeing two men employed in carrying baskets of human bones from the corner of the ground next the old watch-house (where there was a tarpaulin hung over the rails to prevent their being seen, and where they appeared to be heaped up in a mound), to the back of the ground through a small gate. Where this leads I do not know; but I should be glad, through the medium of your invaluable journal to ask, why is this desecration? Sir,- I feel more particularly than many might do, as I have seen twelve of my nearest and dearest relatives consigned to the grave in that ground; and I felt that, perhaps, I might at the moment be viewing, in the basket of skulls which passed before me, those of my own family thus brutally exhumed...[45]

The site was closed in 1850, and in 1855 King's College Hospital demolished the old workhouse and built a new hospital building, which covered a large part of the site. In 1913 W. H. Smith & Son acquired the site, pulled down the hospital building, and replaced it with 'Strand House', which in turn became the British Library of Political and Economic Science in 1978.[46] In 1839, Walker commented that 'the workhouse, at the north-eastern extremity of this ground, has, within the last few weeks, been disused; and the building it appears, is about to be converted into a hospital'. This is where the Royal College of Surgeons now stands.

---

45 See *The Changing Face of Death* pp.87-88
46 G.Howarth and P. Jupp. 'Enon chepel in *The Changing Face of Death: Historical Accounts of Death and Disposal* (199), p.95.

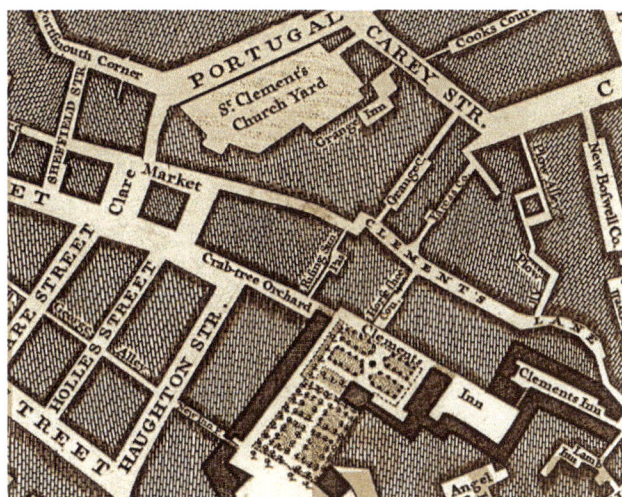

The 1746 Rocque map shows the burial ground on the corner of Portugal and Carey Streets.

The Enon Chapel (underneath LSE), St Clements Building, WC2

The Enon Chapel stood in St Clements Lane, which connects the Strand with Portugal Street. Its exact location was at the southern end of Grange Court, 'just to the north of where it joins St Clements Passage, at the top of the steps down to today's Towers'.[47]

The chapel was a Baptist chapel opened in 1822. The chapel lay in the immediate vicinity of Clare Market, now part of the LSE campus, which Walker describes as being situated 'about midway on the western side of Clements Lane' and being surrounded on all sides by poor housing. This private chapel was to cause a scandal. Knight, in his 1851 London history says that 'all the marvels of the churchyard must give place to those performed in connexion with Enon Chapel. This building is in Clements Lane, in the Strand, and was built by the minister himself (a Dissenter) as a speculation. The upper part, opened for public worship in 1823, is separated from the lower by a boarded floor merely; and in this space (about 60 feet by 29, and 6 deep) 12,000 bodies are estimated to have been interred!'[48] The appalling overcrowding and even worse treatment of the deceased at Enon, according to Knight, came to public attention when

> the Commissioners of Sewers suddenly took it into their heads to compel the minister to arch it over. This was no doubt awkward; but, adapting himself admirably to circumstances, the opportunity was taken of conveying away some sixty loads of mingled earth and human remains, which were shot the other side of Waterloo Bridge, where a pathway was then forming. It may suffice to illustrate the nature of the soil removed, to observe that a few baskets-full having been thoughtlessly given away by the men employed to some labourers executing a slight street repair, a crowd were

---

47 Source: George Kiloh, LSE academic registrar 1996 to 2006, from December 2006 LSE magazine.

48 Knight, p.164

presently found round a human hand. After the stoppage of the conveniences already indicated, a new method would be required at Enon Chapel.[49]

A cabinetmaker, who attended the chapel between 1828 and 1835 and who testified before the Parliamentary Select Committee, stated:

At the time I attended it...there were interments, and the place was in a very filthy state: the smell was most abominable and very injurious; I have frequently gone home myself with a severe headache, which I suppose to have been occasioned by the smell, more particularly in the summer time; also, there were insects, something similar to a bug in shape and appearance, only with wings, about the size of a small bug; I have seen them in the summertime hundreds of them flying about the chapel; I have taken

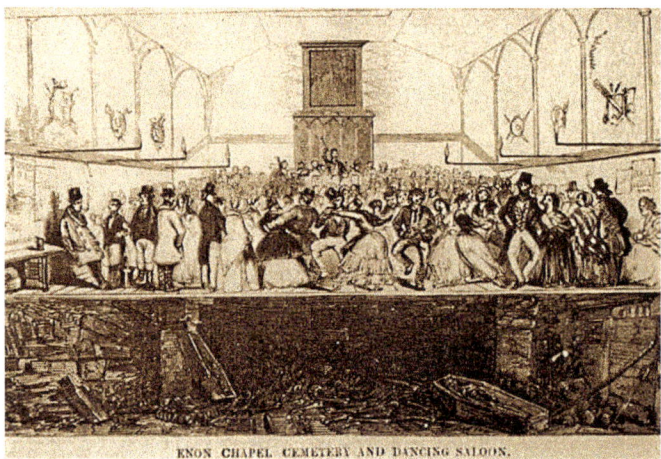

A depiction of the Enon Chapel, the condition of which caused a scandal from the time when it opened in 1823, until closed in 1847. Its former location is under the modern LSE. The print is from *The Poor Man's Guardian*, No. 5, 4 December 1847.

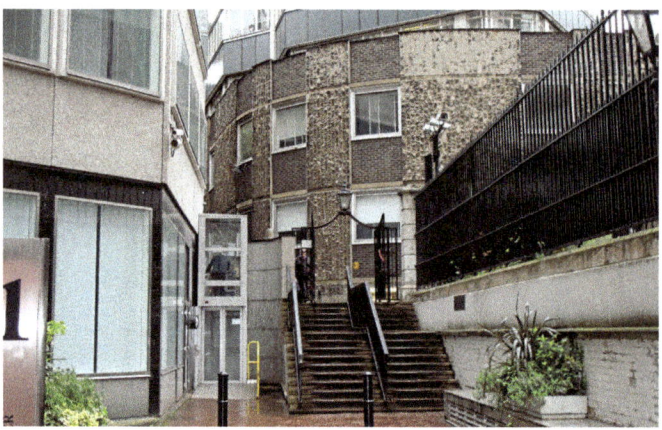

The area at the top of the stairs in Grange Court, where the round building is located is the site of the former Enon Chapel. The chapel was demolished prior to the 1914. O.S. Building works in 1967 produced large quantities of human bones. (Photograph by R. Bard)

---

49 Knight, p.164

them home in my hat, and my wife has taken them home in her clothes; we always considered that they proceeded from the dead bodies underneath.[50]

This chapel was opened for public worship in 1823, the upper part used for worship, and the lower part used for burials: Walker informs us

> this [lower part] is used as a burying place, and is crowded at one end, even to the top of the ceiling, with dead. It is entered from the inside of the chapel by a trap door; the rafters supporting the floor are not even covered with the usual defence – lath and plaster. Vast numbers of bodies (…from ten to twelve thousand bodies) have been placed here in pits, dug for the purpose, the uppermost of which were covered only by a few inches of earth; a sewer runs angularly across this 'burying place'.[51]

Above this seething stench of corruption, insects started to escape into the chapel area where children attended Sunday school. There were graphically described complaints from those who were unfortunate to come within the vicinity of the Enon Chapel, but being private, with a strong profit motive, the burials continued. Walker says:

> I have several times visited this Golgotha. I was struck with the total disregard of decency exhibited, -- numbers of coffins were piled in confusion –large quantities of bones were mixed with the earth, and lying upon the floor of this cellar (for vault it ought not be called), lids of *coffins* might be trodden upon at almost every step….I want language to express the intense feelings of pity, contempt, and abhorrence I experienced…[52]

Foul Abuses
The chapel still notorious enough in 1878 for Walter Thornbury to include reference to its horrors in his London history.

> But far worse than the graveyard alluded to above, [Portugal Street Burial Ground] was another place of burial within the limits of this parish, long known as Enon Chapel, but afterwards converted into a chapel of ease to St. Clements, and called Clare Market Chapel. The building stands close to the eastern entrance to Clements Inn, and the access to it is through a gateway leading into a narrow and extremely dingy court, which opens out into Carey Street. It was converted from secular to religious uses in 1823, by a Dissenting congregation, of whom Mr. Diprose writes—"These pious people, looking very naturally to ways and means, turned the vaults beneath their meeting-house into a burial-place, which soon became

---

50 Quoted from 'Enon Chapel' in Howarth, G. and P. Jupp (1997). *The Changing Face of Death: Historical Accounts of Death and Disposal.* Basingstoke, Macmillan. P.95
51 Walker, p.155
52 Walker, p.157

filled with coffins up to the very rafters, so that there was only the wooden flooring between the living youth and the festering dead, for a Sunday-school was held in the chapel as well as the congregational meeting. This state of things was allowed to continue till 1844, when a new sewer having to be carried under the building, the Commissioners of Sewers discovered the loathsome charnel-house, and had the place closed, but left the bodies to lie there and rot, heedless of all consequences. The upper premises then became tenanted by a set of teetotallers, who, amongst other uses, turned it into a dancing-room, where the thoughtless and giddy went to 'foot it' away over the mouldering remains of sad mortality, part of the bygone generation turning to dust beneath the dancers' feet." This loathsome abomination ceased in 1847–8, when a surgeon, Mr. G. A. Walker, gained possession of the chapel with the intention of removing the remains from the vault, or "dusthole," as it was usually called, to a more appropriate place. The work of exhumation was then commenced, and a pyramid of human bones was exposed to view, separated from piles of coffin wood in various stages of decay. This "Golgotha" was visited by about 6,000 persons, previous to its removal, and some idea may be formed of the horrid appearance of the scene, when it is stated that the quantity of remains comprised four upheaved van loads. The whole mass of bodies was decently interred by Mr. Walker, at his own cost, in one pit in the cemetery at Norwood, the coffin wood being piled up and burnt. It is indeed strange to think that such foul abuses were not swept away until the reign of Victoria.[53]

As late as 1896 the chapel was described by Holmes as 'one of the most notoriously offensive spots in London'.[54] It was built to be profitable and, the burial fees being moderate, was extensively resorted to by the poor as a place of burial. Holmes says that 'no less than 20,000 coffins were deposited here. In order to accomplish this herculean task it was common practice to burn the older coffins in the minister's house, under his copper and in his fireplaces'.[55] After being cleared by Walker, the former chapel was at varying times a concert room, casino, and theatre, becoming known as Clare Market Chapel around 1861.

In 1897 a government laboratory was built on the site. In 1967 the LSE purchased the site for its new St Clements Building and uncovered 'a large quantity of human bones, among them four or five complete skulls'.[56] The exact location of the Enon Chapel was 'at the southern end of the continuation of Grange Court, just a little north of where it joins St Clement's Passage, at the top of the steps down to today's Towers'.[57]

---

53 *St Clement Danes: The parish*, Old and New London: Volume 3 (1878), pp. 26-32.
54 Holmes, p.193
55 Holmes, p.193,194
56 See *The Changing Face of Death* p.103
57 See George Kiloh's article available at http://lse.ac.uk/resources/LSEMagazine/pdf/summer2006/CornerofLondon.pdf

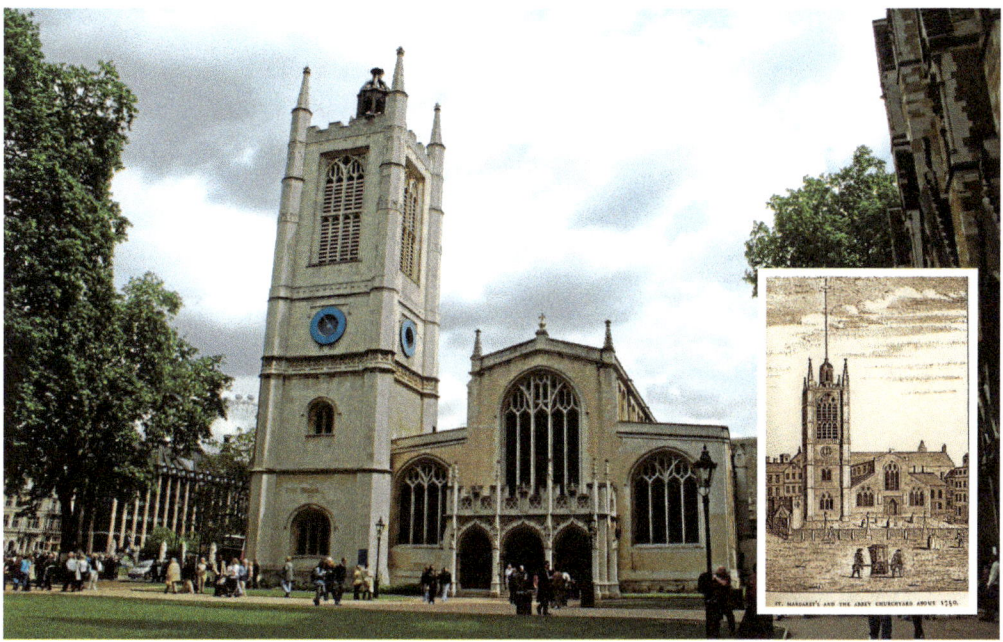

Inset: St Margaret's Churchyard from an illustration of around 1750. The churchyard was full to overflowing and a health hazard. (Illustration from Holmes, 1896)

St Margaret's Churchyard. (Photograph by R. Bard)

St Margaret's Churchyard, Westminster, London, SW1

Revd H. H. Milman, rector of St Margaret's, was questioned in 1843 about how full his nearby churchyard was and whether burials should be continued there. His answer was that it was very full and that no more interments should take place there; not on grounds of health but because of where it was located: 'it is a thoroughfare, and, in point of fact, it has been a cemetery so long, and is so crowded, that interment cannot take place without interfering with previous interments'.[58]

Of the now immaculately kept St Margaret's, which lies a matter of yards from both Westminster Abbey and the Houses of Parliament, Walker says, 'The ground behind the church, is too full to admit of increase, with propriety or safety.' [59]

St James Clerkenwell Additional Ground, Bowling Green Lane, Islington, EC1

The burial ground, situated on the corner of Bowling Green Lane and Clerkenwell Close was in use between around 1660 and 1853. It has now been cleared to allow the development of business and residential buildings. The archaeological contractors

---

58 Chadwick, p.142
59 Walker, p.183

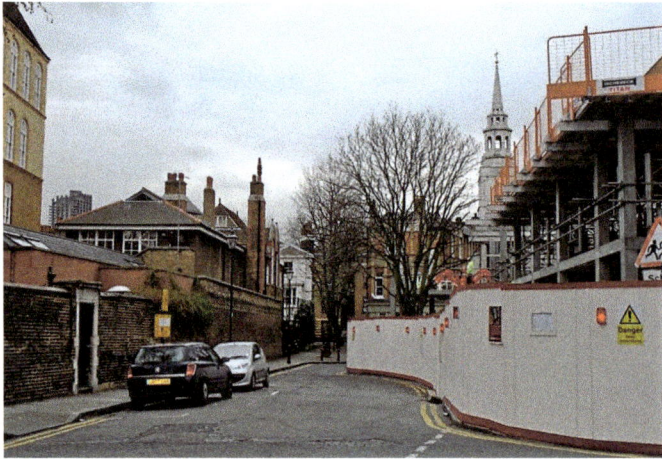

The exhumations took place behind the barricades on the right. In the background is the spire of St James Church showing the relationship of this burial ground, where over 3,000 souls were interred to the church. (Photograph by R. Bard))

called in to observe and supervise the exhumations estimated that at least 3,000 people were buried in the cemetery.[60] Holmes described the ground in 1896 as '¼ acre in size, situated at the corner of Rosoman Street and Bowling Green Lane. The London School Board secured it when the lease ran out, and it is now the playground of the Bowling Green Lane School'.

St Bride's Churchyard, Fleet Street

This churchyard is interesting for a number of reasons, not least that the nearby crypt once contained the remains of Samuel Richardson, whose coffin was discovered in 1993 during archaeological work. There is a fascinating article on the discovery and pathology of Richardson's remains in *Current Archaeology* issue 190 (February 2004). The crypt has now been transformed into a museum, littered with well-preserved tombstones and an iron coffin. The churchyard and its additional ground in Harp Alley were used extensively during the 1665 plague as was the nearby St Dunstans. Vanessa Harding, who has made a study of plague burials, comments that:

> The records of St Bride's also show that at least two of the expedients often considered characteristic of plague burial in London, the organized collection of corpses and the opening of mass graves, were at least to begin with parish initiatives. St Bride's and St Dunstan's jointly employed a party of bearers from July onwards; an early reference to 'slinges to carry the dead corpes', and the absence of any later references to carts suggests that bearing was always done on foot in these parishes. Other parishes, perhaps especially the larger ones, bought or hired carts as they found necessary. It is difficult to discover whether a centralized system of dead-carts ever existed, or whether it was always carried out by parishes, perhaps acting together in groups. Defoe says that 'the dead carts in the city were not confined to particular

---

60 See http://www.aocarchaeology.com/field-archaeology/bowlinggreen.htm

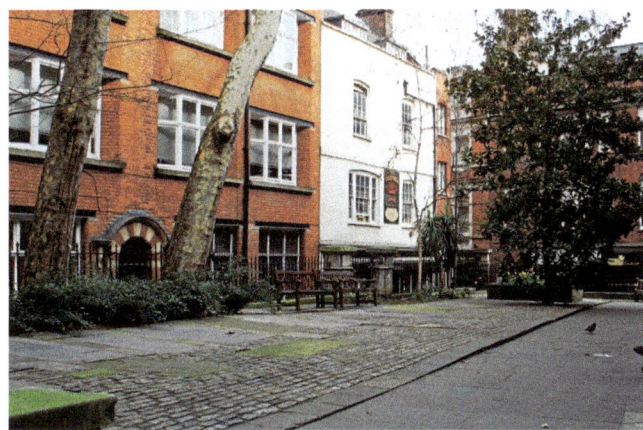

St Bride's Churchyard had pits dug for plague victims in 1665. Note the height of the ground against the surrounding buildings, the result of large numbers of burials over the centuries. (Photograph by R. Bard)

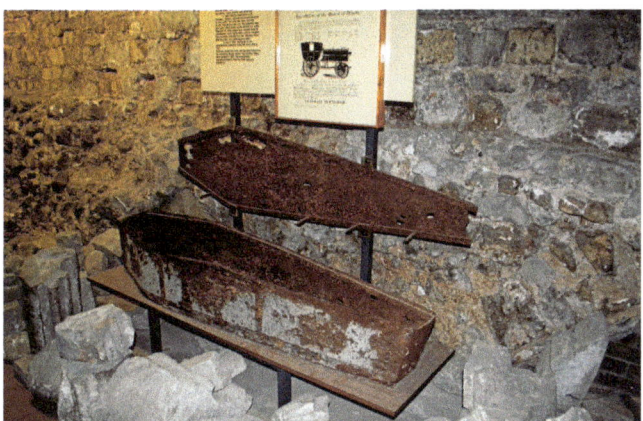

The iron coffin on display in the crypt of St Bride's. It was devised to foil bodysnatchers. In 1820 following a court judgment, they were banned because they took much longer to disintegrate than wooden coffins and space was scarce. (Photograph by R. Bard)

parishes, but one cart went through several parishes, according as the number of dead presented,' but, if this is so, the means by which this was organized and financed is not clear.[61]

In the 1665 plague, at St Dunstan in the West, the first pits were dug in mid-August; at St Bride's, as we have seen, in late August. At St Botolph Aldgate a number of pits were dug in August, but the 'great pit' in the churchyard, and which came to contain over a thousand bodies, received its first corpse on 6 September, according to Defoe's account. 'Some blamed the churchwardens for suffering such a frightful thing ... but time made it appear the churchwardens knew the condition of the parish better than they did': within a fortnight it had been filled up with 1,114 bodies. It seems likely that most, perhaps all, of the larger suburban parishes of London ended by burying their plague dead in mass graves, but that the smaller city-centre parishes did not need to do so. The main motive for digging mass graves was obviously to

---

61 http://www.history.ac.uk/cmh/epiharding.html

accommodate the maximum number of corpses in a small space, but the parishes may also have been driven to it to save money. They were shouldering the massive financial burden of supporting 'visited' families, watching houses, searching and reporting the dead, and by the height of the epidemic the great majority of families could make no contribution to the cost of burial. Though the pits were expensive to dig, taking several days' labour, they were cheap to fill, while individual graves and interments would have been more costly, even had space been available.[62]

About halfway through 1665 plague victims were refused burial at St Bride's. Once the plague had ceased, St Bride's levelled its lower and middle churchyards. The existing churchyard is still extremely high above pavement level.

St Bride's Additional Ground, Harp Alley

The additional ground for St Bride's, known as the lower churchyard, was under a courtyard in the present Harp Alley partly on the site of ground. It is a small alley, easy to miss situated alongside a large taxi rank. In 1991–92 excavations in a small area measuring 12m by 7m at 72–82 Farringdon Street, produced 606 burials, 8 deep, and a communal brick burial vault. Several thousand other burials were reburied in East London Cemetery. A small number of burials still survive below the Hoop & Grapes pub on Farringdon Street. (Site code FAO90, London Archaeologist Round-up 1992 (part 1)). Holmes, in 1896, tells us that the ground 'is off Farringdon Street, is about 750 square yards in extent, and used as a volunteer drill-ground. There are no tombstones, and the ground is untidy. Consecrated 1610. Given by the Earl of Dorset'.

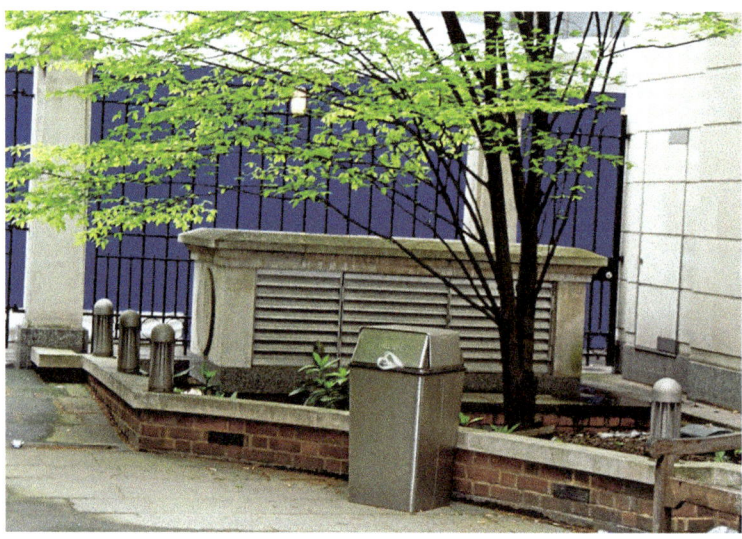

Courtyard in Harp Alley where burials from the nearby St Bride's Church lay. (Photograph by Les Abrahams.)

---

62 http://www.history.ac.uk/cmh/epiharding.html

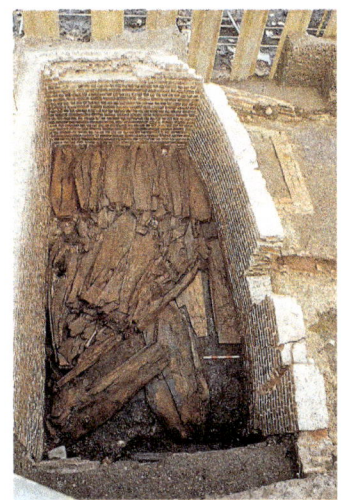

The communal vault at St Bride's lower churchyard, Harp Alley. (Photograph ©MOLA)

St Giles-in-the-Fields Churchyard, St Giles High Street, WC2

Holmes says that 'the churchyard of St Giles' in the Fields is a very interesting one'. Writing in the last decade of the nineteenth century, she comments that the church should really be called 'St Giles' in the Slums'. She comments that the practices carried out in the churchyard at the beginning of the nineteenth century 'were equal to the worst anywhere – revolting ill-treatment of the dead was the daily custom'.[63] Walker, quoting from Pennant[64] in 1813, writes,

> I have in the church yard of St.Gile's, seen with horror, a great square pit, with many rows of coffins piled one upon the other, all exposed to sight and smell; some of the piles were incomplete, expecting the mortality of the night. I turned away disgusted at the view, and scandalized at the want of police...[65]

Walker reproduces an extract from the *Weekly Dispatch* of 30 September 1838:

> St.Giles's Church Yard. – What horrid place is Saint Giles's church yard! It is full of coffins, up to the surface. Coffins are broken up before they are decayed, and bodies are removed to the 'bone house' before they are sufficiently decayed to make their removal decent. The effect upon the atmosphere, in that very densely populated spot, must be very injurious. I had occasion to attend the church with several gentlemen, on Tuesday; being required to wait, we went into this Golgotha; near the east side we saw a finished grave, into which had projected a nearly sound coffin; half of the coffin

---

63 Holmes, p.108
64 Pennant, T. (1813). Some account of London, Westminster and Southwark: illustrated with numerous views. London, p.157
65 Walker, p.164,165

had been chopped away to complete the shape of the new grave. A man was standing by with a barrowful of sound wood, and several bright coffin plates. I asked him 'Why is all this?' and his answer was, 'O, it is all Irish'. We then crossed to the opposite corner, and there is the 'bone house,' which is a large round pit; into this had been shot, from a wheelbarrow, the partly-decayed inmates of the smashed coffins. Here, in this place of 'Christian burial,' you may see human heads, covered with hair; and here, in this 'consecrated ground,' are human bones with flesh still adhering to them. On the north side, a man was digging a grave; he was quite drunk, so indeed were all the grave diggers we saw. We looked into this grave, but the stench was abominable. We remained however, long enough to see that a child's coffin, which had stopped the man's progress, had been cut, longitudinally, right in half; and there lay the child which had been buried in it, wrapped in its shroud, resting upon the part of the coffin which remained. The shroud was but little decayed. I make no comments; every person must see the ill effects is such practices are allowed to continue.[66]

The churchyard of St Giles-in-the-Fields sits in the immediate vicinity of the gallows that once stood in the vicinity of the main door of the church, and contains the remains of many who were executed, in particular, some that died at nearby Tyburn.

Spa Fields Burial Ground, Rosoman Place, Islington, EC1

Spa Fields is a disjointed area today, compact and gloomy and set in an area surrounded by flats and grey buildings. The ground near the chapel undulates in an alarming manner, suggestive of its former role as one of London's most notoriously overcrowded burial grounds. In 1777 speculators leased 2 acres of ground from the Marquis of Northampton. It was calculated that this would provide space for 2,722 adults, but with burials taking place at 1,500 per annum the ground after fifty years was believed to contain around 80,000 bodies. By 1842, an early London history tells us

> some terrible disclosures began to ooze out, proving the shameless greediness of the human ghouls who farmed the Spa Fields burial-ground. It was found that it was now the nightly custom to exhume bodies and burn the coffins, to make room for fresh arrivals. To make the new grave seven or eight bodies were actually chopped up, and corpses recently interred were frequently dragged up by ropes, so that the coffin might be removed and split up for struts to prop up the new-made graves. Bodies were sometimes destroyed after only two days' burial. A grave-digger who, being discharged, insisted on removing the body of his child, which had been recently interred, declared that he and his mates had buried as many as forty-five bodies in one day, besides still-borns. In one year they had had 2,017 funerals, and the stones of families who had purchased graves in perpetuity were frequently displaced and destroyed. The inhabitants of the neighbourhood then petitioned Parliament, complaining of the infectious smells from the burial ground, and of the shameful

---

66 Walker, p.165,166

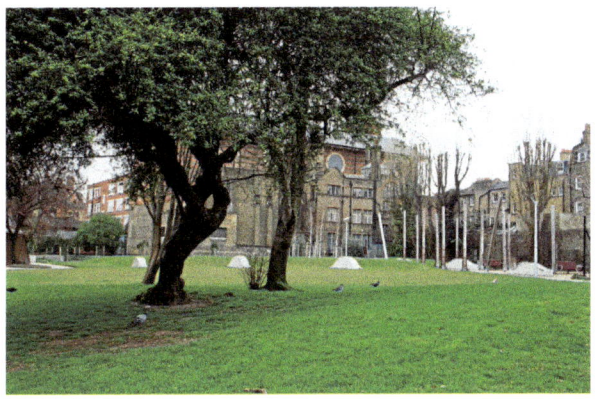

The former burial ground of Spa Fields where around 80,000 persons were buried in the most appalling conditions. This ground caused a scandal. The original chapel was built in 1770. This chapel on the same site dates from *c.* 1887. (Photograph by R. Bard)

scandal generally...On the night of the 14th December, 1843, an alarm was raised that the bone-house of Spa Fields ground was on fire, and the engine-keeper stated he saw in the grate a rib-bone and other bones, partly burnt, and a quantity of coffin-wood in different stages of decay. By the exertions of Mr. G. A. Walker, MD., of the Society for the Abolition of Burials in Towns, seconded by several of the principal inhabitants, this disgraceful state of things was brought again under the attention of the magistrates, and the lessees, managers, and others were summoned to appear at the Clerkenwell Police Court, when other revolting statements were made and confirmed. At length these disgusting and loathsome practices were suppressed by law.[67]

Walker says that 'this ground was originally taken for a tea garden; the speculation failed, and a chapel was built upon it, in which some ministers of the Church of England preached ... The burying ground is very large, but absolutely saturated with dead ... This place offers a difficult problem for solution; – no undertaker can explain it, except by a shrug of the shoulders. I can affirm, from frequent personal observation, that enormous numbers of dead have been deposited here'. Knight, writing in 1841, observes that a parliamentary report in 1814 stated of the overflowing Spa Fields that there was 'no more space, but that you can always get a grave there', Knights adds, 'any graves for not less than thirty or forty persons weekly, that being frequently the number of interments'.[68]

By 1896, when Mrs Holmes was suggesting that disused burial grounds be turned into recreation areas. Her description of the ground and surrounding area is a reminder that appalling conditions in London were not uncommon, even at the end of the nineteenth century. She comments that Spa Fields

was now a typical London playground which was 'in the very centre of the town, although surrounded by courts and streets with such rural names as Rosoman Street,

---

67 *Coldbath Fields and Spa Fields*, Old and New London: Volume 2 (1878), pp. 298-306.
68 Knight, p.168

Wood Street, Pear-tree Court and Vineyard Walk – grim reminders of what the district was like a hundred years or more ago. Exmouth Street, behind which this open space is situated, is worth a visit. I was there recently, one Monday afternoon. Trucks and stalls with wares of all kinds lined the narrow road, and there seemed scarcely a square yard without a person on it. One woman was selling old garments, of which she had only about six, and these were spread out on the road itself – in the mud...In the middle of the street is the Church of the Holy Redeemer, a huge structure in imitation of an Italian church. It stands on the site of the Spa Fields Chapel, an old round building, removed a few years ago...behind the church is the open space, which is nearly two acres in extent. Originally taken for a tea-garden the speculation failed, and the ground was used as a burial-ground, slightly lower fees being charged than in the neighbouring churchyards. After being grossly overcrowded it was closed for interments in 1853. For several years the space has been used as a drill-ground by the 3rd Middlesex Rifles; and in 1885 the Metropolitan Public Gardens Association entered into negotiations with the owner, the Marquis of Northampton, and he generously handed it over at a nominal rental for the purposes of a children's playground and subsequently added to it half an acre of adjoining land.[69]

Having visited the ground and watched the children of the poor playing in 'tattered clothes' in the dull and grey setting of the now children's playground, she asks, 'can the dead beneath the soil object to the little feet above them? I am sure they cannot ... Such a space as Spa Fields may never have been consecrated for the use of the dead, but perchance the omission is in part redeemed by its dedication to the living'.[70]

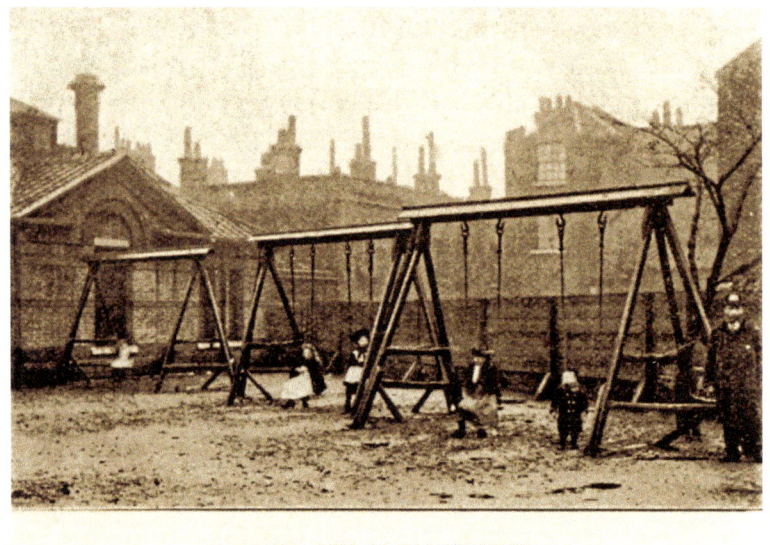

A late nineteenth-century photograph of poor children playing in Spa Fields. (From Holmes)

---

69 Holmes, 274, 275
70 Holmes, p.278

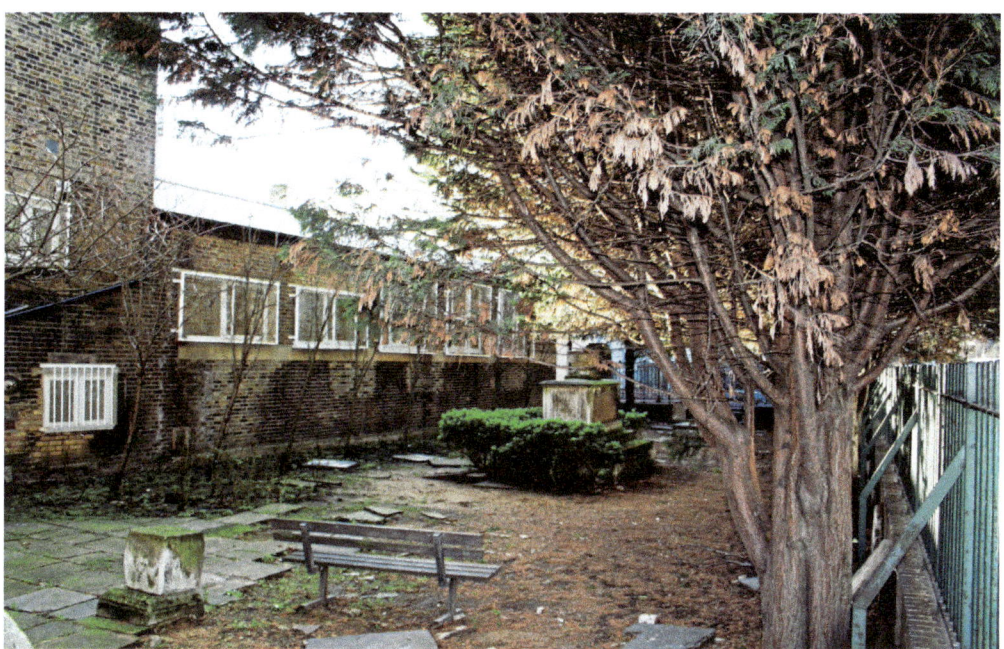

The Globe Road Memorial Gardens. The scene of some of the worst events in nineteenth-century burial ground records. A dreadful stench emanated from this ground and the deceased rarely remained at peace for more than a few days before making way for newcomers. It was from the vicinity of the railway that, in 1839, a railway employee noticed coffins being disturbed and bones stolen from this yard. (Photograph by R. Bard)

Globe Fields, Whitechapel (Now Globe Road Memorial Gardens), E2

The Globe Fields burial ground remains today, in truncated form, as a mute testimony to one of the worst burial ground scandals of the nineteenth century. In a testimony before a Parliamentary Select Committee of 1842, the ground was described as being half an acre in extent. In 1896, Holmes writes that 'over half of the Globe Fields ground the Great Eastern Railway runs; the remainder is a bare yard, with several miserable tomb-stones in it and quantities of rubbish. It is fast closed behind an iron gate of colossal proportions, and it daily becomes more neglected and untidy'.[71]

The ground is still untidy and neglected. The gates are locked but the ground is easily visible from Globe Road.

A *Morning Post* article of Monday 14 October 1839 says of this burial ground:

INDECENT DISINTERMENT OF DEAD BODIES

Since Friday, a good deal of excitement has prevailed in the neighbourhood of Globe Lane, Mile-end, in consequence of the interference of the police to prevent

---

71 Holmes, pp.197-198

the indecent disinterment of bodies in the burial ground behind Globe Fields Chapel. It appeared that Mr. Poole, a clerk in the service of the Eastern Counties Railway Company, being stationed on that part of the railroad which runs close to the burial ground in question, had observed two men and a boy exhuming the bodies buried in one part of the ground, and hurling them, in the most indecent manner, and indiscriminately, into a deep hole, which they had previously made at another part; and considering such a proceeding as somewhat extraordinary, as well as exceedingly indecent, he felt it to be his duty to call at the police station-house, in the Mile-end Road, and give information of what he had witnessed. Inspector M'Craw, accompanied by sergeants Parker and Shaw....proceeded to the burial ground in question, and as they were about to enter, they met a lad with a bag of bones and a quantity of nails, which he said he was going to sell. On examining them, the nails were evidently those which had been taken out of coffins, and the bones seemed to be those of human beings, but the lad denied that they were so, though he acknowledged the nails to have been taken from the coffins. The inspector and sergeants then proceeded to an obscure corner of the ground, and found there a great number of bodies, packed one upon another, in a very deep grave which had been dug to receive them, and the uppermost coffin was not more than seven or eight inches, at the utmost, from the surface. The breast-plate and nails were removed from the lid, so that they could at once remove the latter, and from the appearance of the body, as well as of the coffin, it appeared to be the remains of a person above the middle ranks of life, and to have been interred about a month or six weeks.

The Friends' Burial Ground, Bunhill Row, EC1

This ground is located off Bunhill Row, and is not immediately obvious. The Memorial Building mentioned by Holmes is still there, and the remaining portion is now a small park and playground with several memorials. The ground is atmospheric and peaceful. Holmes says of this ground that it was 'acquired in 1661, many times added to, and chiefly used by the Friends of the Peel and Bull-and-Mouth divisions. In 1840 a school was

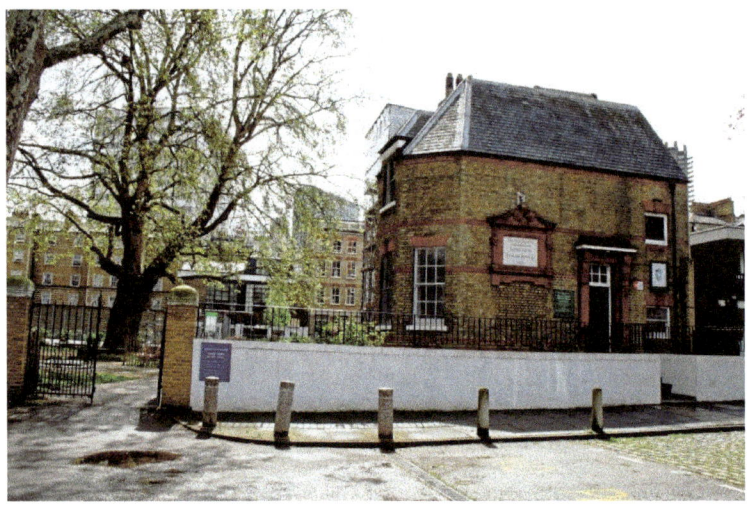

Entrance to the Friends' Burial Ground, Bunhill Row. (Photograph by R. Bard)

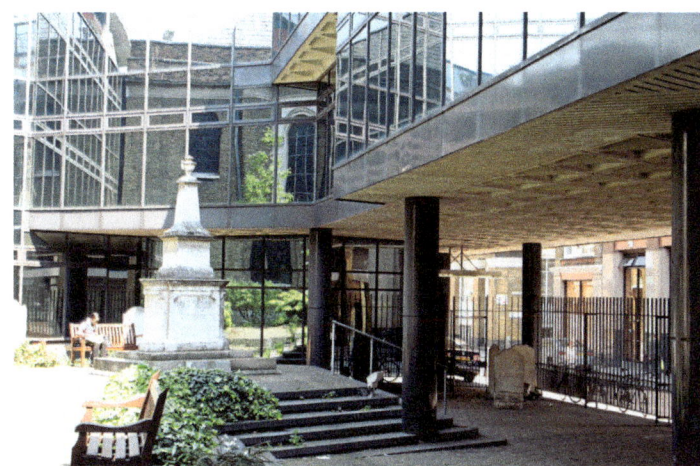

The office block is raised over the burial ground. (Photograph by R. Bard)

built in it. The existing portion is about ½ acre in size, and is neatly kept as a private garden; but the remainder was used as the site for a Board School, a coffee palace, houses and shops, including the Bunhill Fields Memorial Buildings, erected in 1881.'[72]

Wesleyan Chapel Ground, City Road, EC1

This ground is an unusual combination of churchyard, office block, and recreation ground. Access is opposite the City Road entrance to Bunhill Fields at the back of Wesley's Chapel, which is worth a visit for the free museum alone. The ground is tidy, with a number of gravestones protruding from concrete underneath the entrance to an office block. The large monument is the site where Wesley and others are buried. Holmes commented in 1896 that it was '½ acre. The part in front of the chapel is neatly kept, but the part behind is closed and not so tidy. Wesley himself was buried in a vault here'.

Poor Ground, Bath Street, EC1

This former burial ground of the Pesthouse, which stood almost opposite in Bath Street, is still open ground surrounded on three sides by blocks of flats and playground equipment. The area is also a pedestrian cut-through. There are no reminders of the former ground.

'This was originally larger than it is now. It was consecrated in 1662 for the parish of St Giles, Cripplegate, and called the pest-house ground. After 1732, when St. Luke's parish was formed, it was used by that parish. Now it is neatly laid out and used as a recreation ground by the patients of the St Luke's Asylum. It is ¼ acre in extent.' (Holmes) There were other burial grounds, also lost, in Bath Street, known in earlier centuries as Pesthouse Row. There was the French Hospital Burial Ground, which stood on the site the Pesthouse. When the hospital was moved in 1866, the bodies were removed to the City of London Cemetery. Holmes does not mention this ground.

---

[72] Holmes, p. 291.

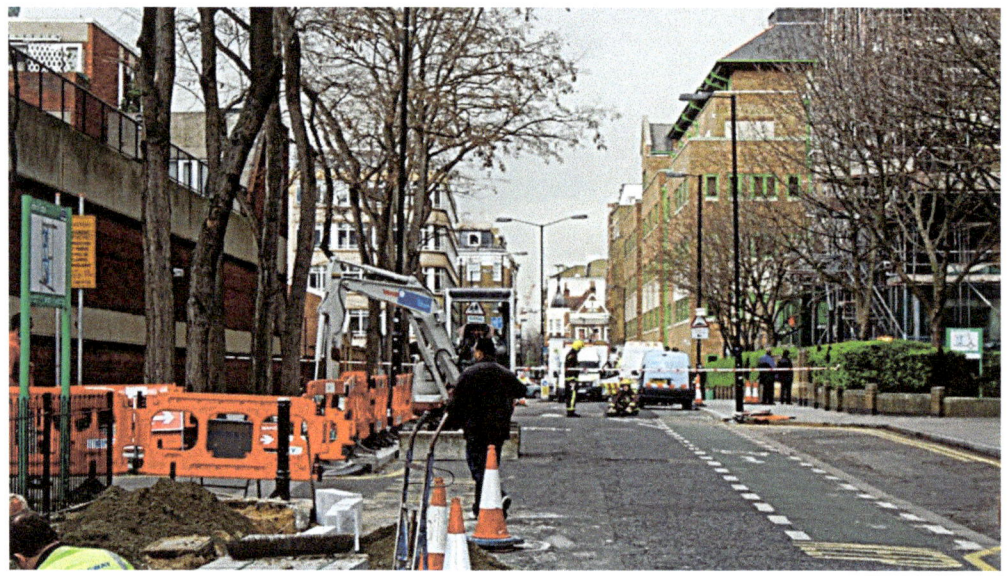

The site of Bath Street Pest House on the left. A green London Borough of Islington plaque on the red-brick wall of a modern building reads: 'City Pesthouse: Built here in open fields 1593. Used during the Great Plague 1665. Demolished 1736.' The burial ground is on an estate on the right. (Photograph by R. Bard)

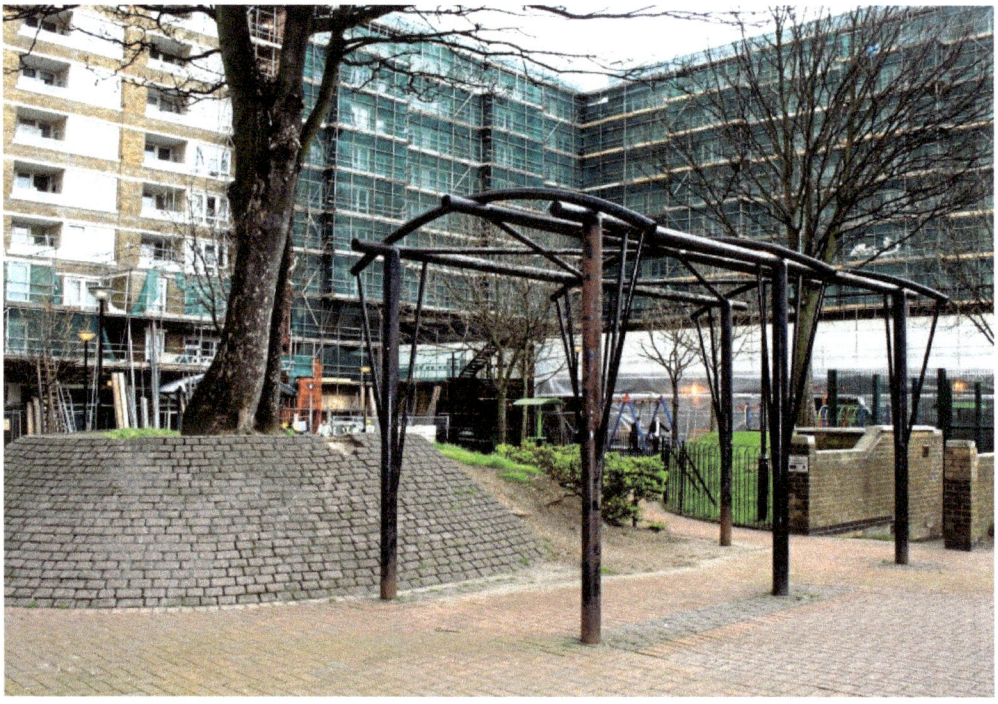

Consecrated in 1662, this area of the St Luke's Estate was the burial ground for the pesthouse that was situated almost opposite in Bath Street. (Photograph by R. Bard)

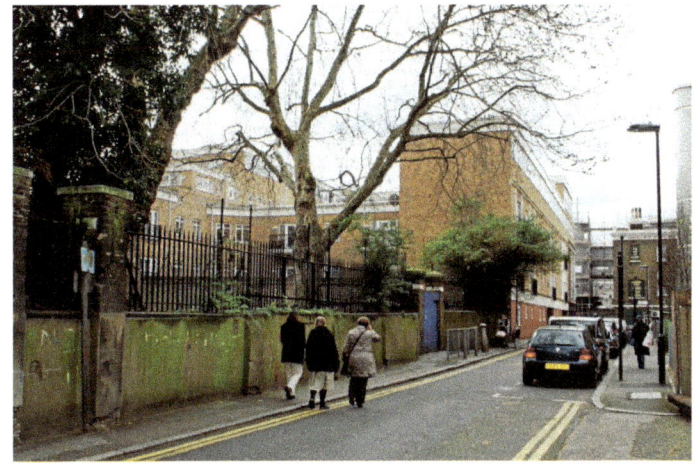

On the left behind the railings, now closed up, is a former children's playground that sits on the site of a burial ground, which was used in earlier centuries by St Bartholomew's Hospital for the burial of unclaimed bodies. At the bottom of the street to the right of the photograph is Mount Mills, a 1665 plague pit. (Photograph by R. Bard)

St Bartholomew's Hospital Ground, Seward Street, EC1

This burial ground may have been used during the 1665 plague, but was, Holmes tells us, used for the interment of the unclaimed bodies generated by St Bartholomew's Hospital. The area of burial, around half an acre, was laid out as a public playground in 1891. It is now closed up and derelict. It is situated a matter of yards from the Mount Mills plague pit.

The City Bunhill (or Golden Lane) Burial Ground, EC1

This burial ground lies underneath the new Golden Lane Campus School off Whitecross Street. The school is located alongside the Fortune Gardens. The City Bunhill burial ground was a Nonconformist burial ground, in use from October 1833 until its closure on 14 August 1853. During this period, the burial registers show that at least 18,036 burials took place. A sample area approximately 15m by 10m was excavated archaeologically in 2006, from which a total of 248 burials were recovered.[73]

The other surviving bodies were exhumed and reinterred in St Pancras and Islington Cemetery, East Finchley. The burial ground was divided into three sections – Upper, Middle and Lower – with differing charges for burial. The excavated area was located within the Lower ground, the cheapest of these. Burial took place in alphanumerically identified plots, which were for general use, not family plots. The plot information can be found within the burial registers, which also contain data concerning the time of burial and the undertaker, along with the name, date, age and address at the time of death. This information has been used to examine the buried population and the use of the burial ground. The great majority of burials took place on a Sunday, all carried out in the afternoon, between 2 p.m. and 4.30 p.m. The burial

---

73 Connell, B, and Miles, A, 2010 The City Bunhill burial ground, Golden Lane: Excavations at South Islington Schools, 2006 MOLA Archaeology studies series 21, London

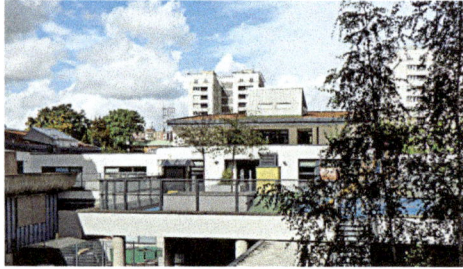

Left: The City Bunhill excavation area was below the new academy building. (Photograph by A. Miles)

Below: Coffins being recorded during the excavations at City Bunhill, 2006, showing typical nineteenth-century coffin construction. (©MOLA)

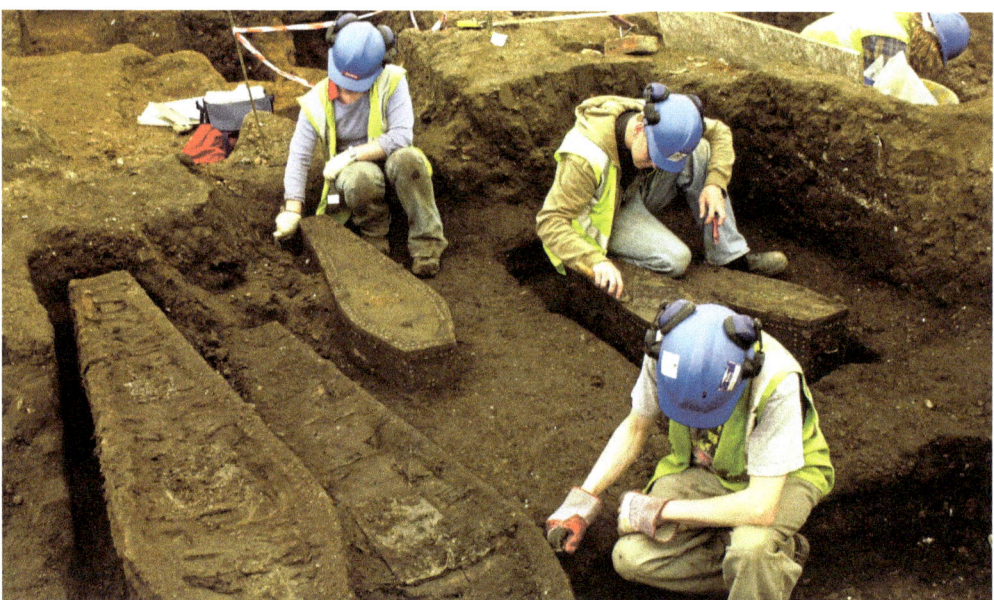

ground is identifiable on the 1873 Ordnance Survey map. Holmes mentions the site as being a burial ground of

> 1¼ acres. This was the site of a brewery, and set aside for burials in 1833. About one-third of it is in the City. It is now divided. One part is in the occupation of Messrs. Sutton and Co., carriers, and is full of sheds and carts, the greater part being roofed in, and the southern part has the City mortuary and coroner's court on it. What is unbuilt upon is a neat, private yard between these two buildings. It was closed for burials in 1853.[74]

Cripplegate Poor Ground, Whitecross Street and Thomas' Golden Lane, EC1

Both of these grounds now lie under the Peabody Estate, no more than 500 yards from the Golden Lane Campus. David Orme suggests the Cripplegate Poor-ground (not shown on Rocque or Horwood) lies under the central open area of the Peabody Estate.

---

74 Holmes, p291-2

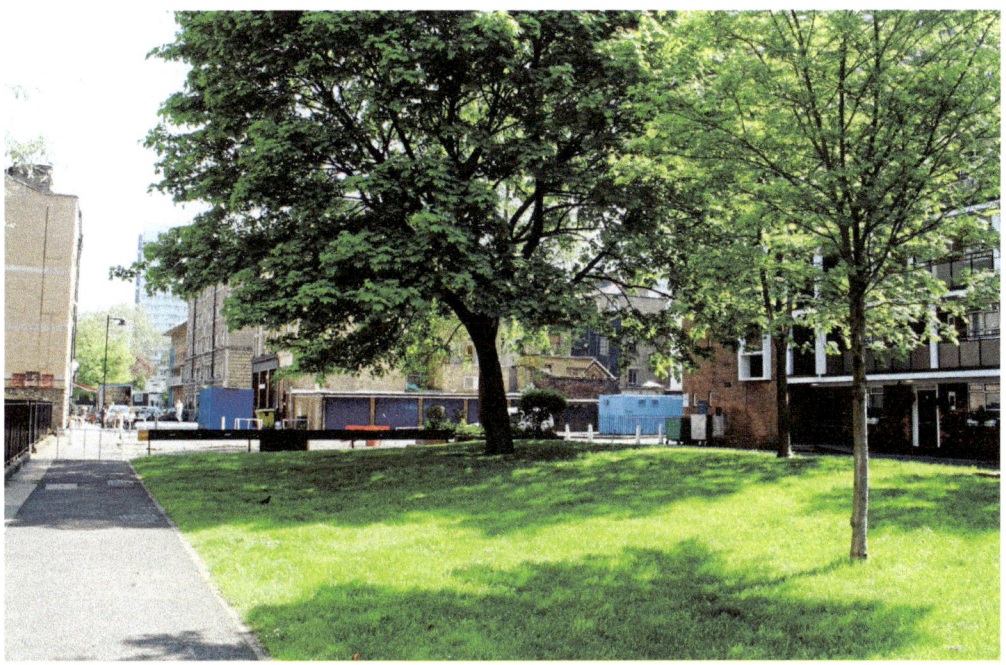

Central area of the Peabody Estate covers a burial ground first used in 1636. (Photograph by R. Bard)

Holmes says of this ground that, 'It was called the 'upper churchyard' of St Giles, and was first used in 1636. It was very much overcrowded, the fees being low. A part of the site is occupied by the church and mission-house of St Mary, Charterhouse, erected in 1864. And only a very small courtyard now exists between these buildings, with a large vault.'

Islington Chapel Ground, Formerly Church Street and now Gaskin Street, N1

This ground, also known as Little or New Bunhill Fields, was originally known as Jones's Burial Ground after the Revd Evan Jones, who purchased a garden in 1817 to add to the small existing graveyard. The ground was cleared by commercial contractors in 1996 when the site was being redeveloped.

An archaeological watching brief monitored the works to try and identify any patterns and to collect any surviving coffin furniture. It showed that the graves were laid out in neat rows, with burials stacked up to seven deep within each grave, and there were brick vaults for the wealthier individuals. 1,493 coffin plates were recovered, most of which were made from tin-dipped iron, which form a very important collection, unique in this country. The remains were reburied in Islington's Trent Park Cemetery at Cockfosters. (Site code.IGN96, London Archaeologist Round-up 1996.)

The east side of the ground has now been built on, and the west side is now a pleasant garden. Holmes, in 1896, says this ground was also called Little Bunhill Fields and that,

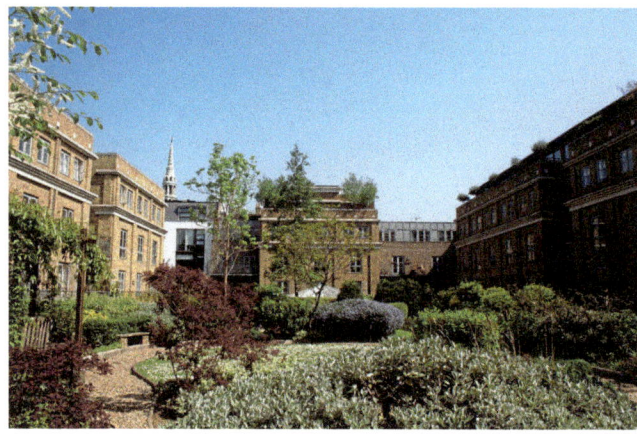

The ground formerly known as 'Little Bunhill Fields' is now Anderson Square. (Photograph by R. Bard)

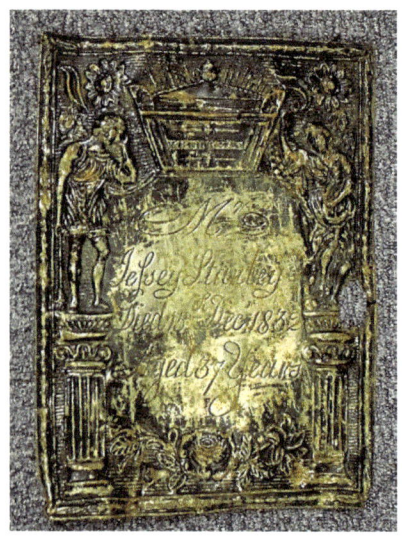

One of many tin-dipped iron coffin plates from New Bunhill Fields, Islington. This one reads: 'Jessey Stanley, died 15 December 1832, aged 37'. (©MOLA)

The original chapel was built in 1788, and had a small graveyard. In 1817 the Rev. Evan Jones bought the garden of 5, Church Row, and added it to this graveyard, the whole ground being nearly 1 acre in extent. It is now in several divisions, part is a yard belonging to the General Post Office, and the other parts are let and sold as builders' yards, or are vacant.[75]

Wesleyan Chapel Ground, originally Liverpool Street, now Liverpool Road, N1

This former burial ground is located in front of the former chapel, now part of the Design Centre to which it is attached. The location of the burial ground itself is most

---

75 Holmes, p.290

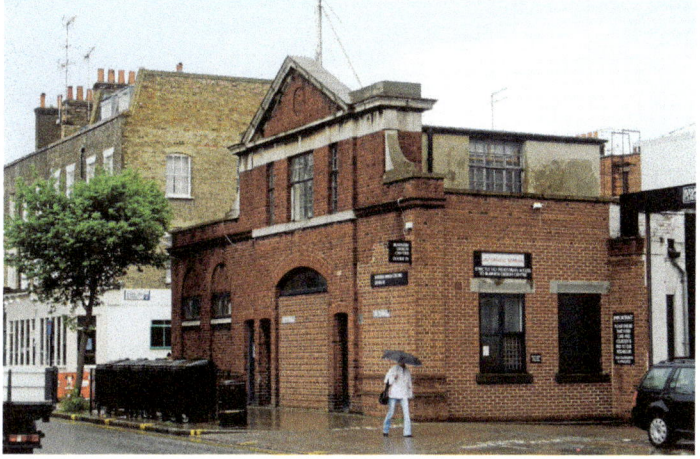

The former Wesleyan Chapel ground, which was described in 1896 as 'containing two tombstones and much rubbish'. The burial ground lies partially under the road and where the black bins are situated. (Photograph by R.Bard)

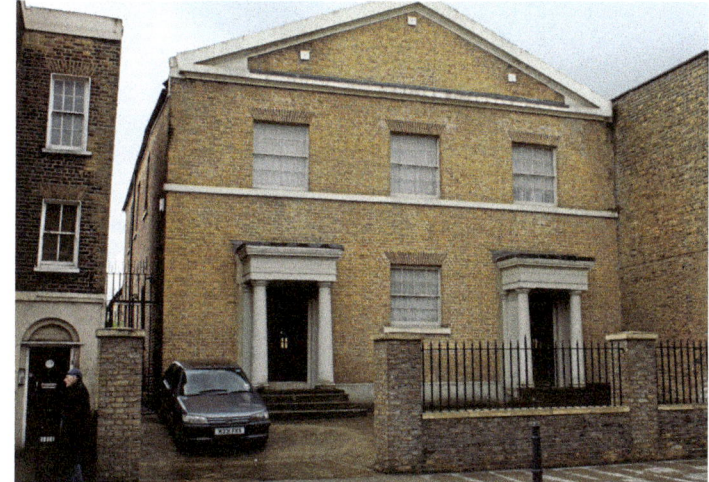

The site of the former Maberley Chapel ground in Ball's Pond Road. The burial area was between 'the chapel and the road'. (Photograph by Les Abrahams)

likely to be the area in front of the chapel where the dustbins in the photograph are located, and partially under the road. Holmes, in 1896, describes the ground as 'an untidy little closed yard at the west end of the chapel containing two tombstones and much rubbish, and measuring 'about 225 square yards'.

Maberley Chapel Ground, Ball's Pond Road, N1

Holmes, in 1896, describes this burial ground formerly called Earlham Hall as being 'about 270 square yards, between the chapel and the road. It is closed and bare.'[76] Now the burial ground is located in front of the restored buildings in the car parking area of 47a Ball's Pond Road.

---

76 Holmes, p.290

St Martin-in-the-Fields Burial Ground, Pratt Street, (now St Martin's Gardens) Camden

This ground, where an estimated 18,000 burials are recorded, was purchased by St Martin-in-the-Fields in 1805 and remained in use until 1856. The ground is not easy to locate, and is situated as a public garden behind the now closed St Martin's Tavern.

There are explanatory notices near the entrance and the large open space is atmospheric. It still contains many tombstones stacked round the walls and some table tombs. Immediately behind the tavern is a quiet, overgrown section of burial ground. An addendum in the copy of Holmes' *London Burial Grounds* leant to the author has this writing about the back of this ground: 'Half way down Pratt Street is the St Martin's Tavern, with the churchyard garden of St Martin's on one side … when the air-raid shelters were being dug, the excavation found so many bodies buried here that the work had to be abandoned.'

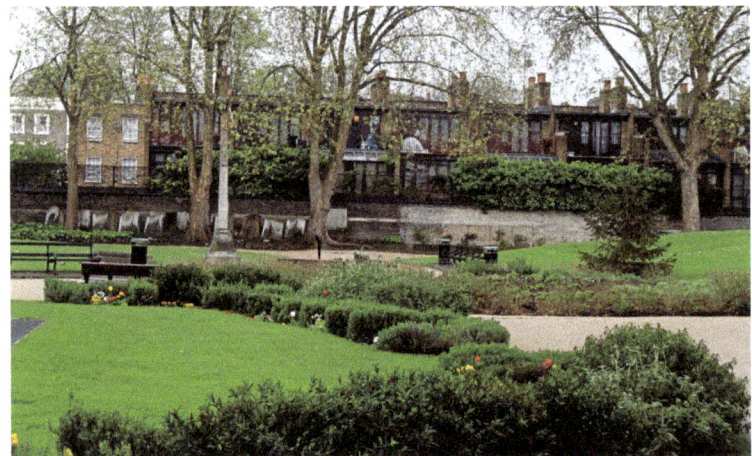

St Martin-in-the-Fields burial ground in Pratt Street (now St Martin's Gardens), Camden. (Photograph by R. Bard)

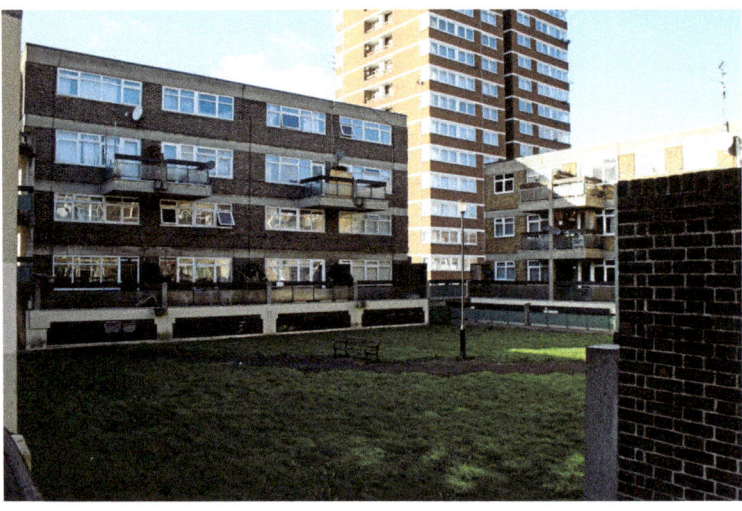

One of the most poignant lost burial grounds. The cemetery lies under the courtyard garden of a low-rise block of flats, almost directly opposite the former hospital. (Photograph by R. Bard)

Aske's Hospital, Edward Dodd Court, Chart Street, Hackney, N1 – Burial Ground of Haberdasher's Almshouses and Schools, Hoxton

This former burial ground is haunting in its anonymity and proximity to the former Aske's Hospital building, which is situated diagonally on the other side of the road in Chart Street. The ground was used for the burial of deceased patients as well as others. The ground is shown on an 1872 Ordnance Survey map. The ground is situated in the courtyard of a low-rise block of flats, on the left, just before Chart Street makes a dogleg to the right.

Friend's Burial Ground, Baker's Row, E1

This former burial ground is now an innocuous East End square, now called Vallance Gardens, in Vallance Road, Whitechapel. This ground is referred to by Holmes in 1896 as being, 'Very nearly an acre. It belonged to the Friends of the Devonshire House division, who acquired it in 1687. It is leased by the society to the Whitechapel District

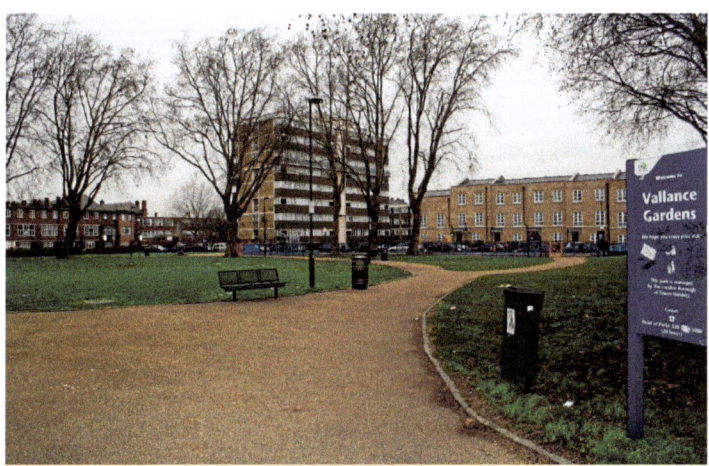

Vallance Gardens, the site of a Quaker burial ground, formerly known as Baker's Row. (Photograph by R. Bard)

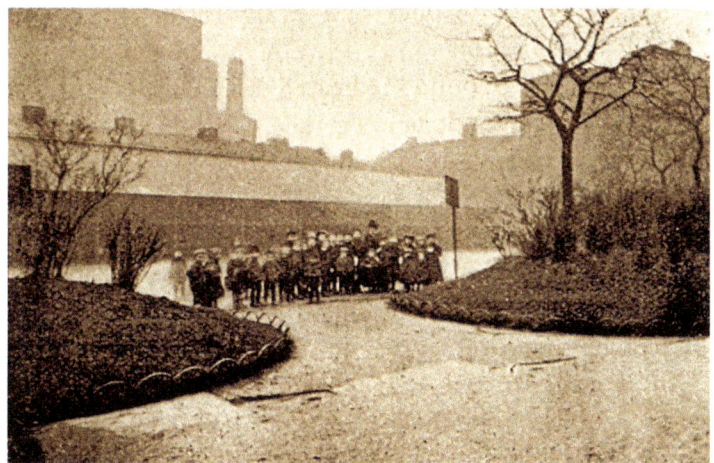

The same view as above, c. 1896. (Photograph from Holmes)

Board of Works, who maintain it as a public recreation ground. It is well laid out and well kept, being chiefly used by children.'[77]

Aldgate Burial Ground, Cartwright Street, Royal Mint Square, E1

This burial ground is located in Cartwright Street, just off East Smithfield near the former Royal Mint. The road is completely residential apart from the recreation ground. There is no indication that the open grassy area is actually a former burial ground. The ground belonged to the parish of St Botolph, Aldgate, and was consecrated in 1615. It went out of use at the end of the eighteenth century. Holmes tells us that at the beginning of the nineteenth century

> it was covered with small houses, the Weigh House School being built on it in 1846. The rookery was cleared by the Metropolitan Board of Works, and Darby Street was made, gravestones and remains being then discovered. The Metropolitan Public Gardens Association informed the Board of the former existence of a burial-ground, with the result that what remained of the burial-ground was not built upon, but was made into an asphalted playground, about 1 acre in extent, for the children of the adjoining block of tenements. [78]

Part of the area was excavated by the Museum of London Archaeology in 2005 during landscaping of the site and it unearthed 238 burials. This was only a small part of the burial ground with the large part still undisturbed. Most of the graves contained more

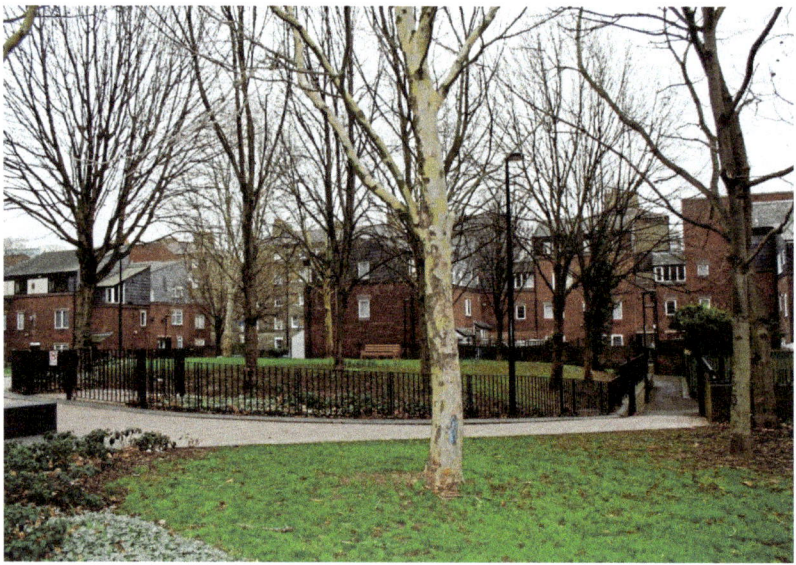

This area is a burial ground that was due to be developed in the nineteenth century, but the discovery of bones led to the ground being asphalted for recreation. (Photograph by R. Bard)

---

77 Holmes, p.297
78 Holmes, p.296

than two burials, some containing four or five. It was used by the poorer members of the parish, the fees being significantly cheaper than those in the main churchyard. [79]

St Katherine's Dock, Next to Tower Bridge, E1

This area is now occupied by shops, flats and the marina, but it once contained two large burial grounds. Today, nothing remains of these former times.

Holmes tells us that

> when St. Katharine's Docks were made, in 1827, St. Katharine's Church, the ruins of the hospital (dating from 1148), two churchyards of considerable size, and the whole parish, -- inns, streets, houses and all, were totally annihilated....It is said that a quantity of the human remains from the churchyard were used to fill up some old reservoirs, &c., in the neighbourhood; but at any rate, it is a fact that they were distributed amongst the East-end churchyards, and several cartloads were taken to Bethnal Green and deposited in St. Matthew's ground where the slope up to the west door of the church is composed of these bodies from St. Katherine's. There were

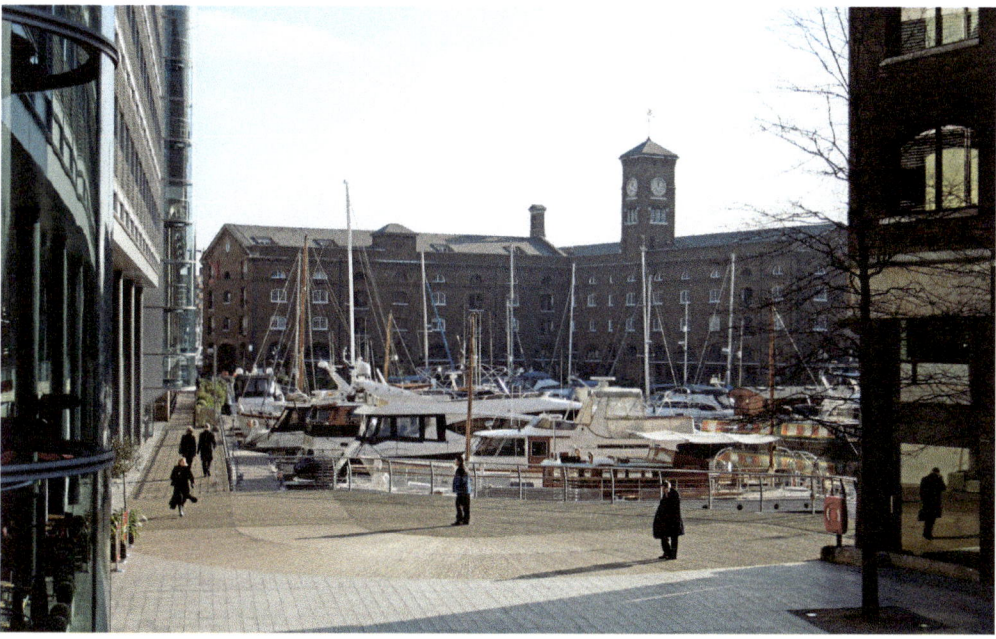

St Katherine's Dock, the former site, contained two churchyards. When the docks were built in 1827, cartloads of human remains were taken away. Many were reinterred at the nearby St Matthew's, where the results can still be seen. The area in the foreground was originally part of St Katherine's churchyard. (Photograph by R. Bard)

---

79 Excavations at Royal Mint Square (Adrian Miles and Jelena Bekvalac) *London Archaeologist* Vol 14, No 2, 2014, 31-36

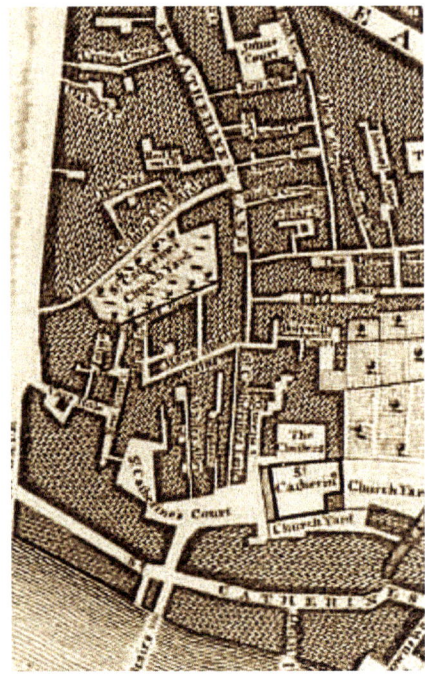

The 1746 Rocque map. The Tower of London moat lies immediately to the west.

originally steps leading to the entrance, but the steps are buried under this artificial hill, the ground having been raised several inches.[80]

The Tower Hotel is situated at the bottom left-hand quarter of the where Rocque shows the area bounded by St Katherine's Court.

New Road Congregational Chapel Yard, Cannon Street Road

This survives as an open area on the Bigland Estate. Archaeological work in 2005 was used to define where the eastern boundary of the burial ground was, which was in use from around 1790. This allowed development to be located only in areas outside the burial ground. No human remains were removed. (Site code BXE05, London Archaeologist Round-up 2005.)

Holmes notes that,

> This was a much-used burial-ground, part of which has been covered with sheds and houses. What is left is about 1/3 acre in extent. The chapel was bought in 1831, and became Trinity Episcopal Chapel, and was subsequently removed and its site used for the new building of Raine's School. The burial-ground is in three parts, viz., the playground of the school, a cooper's yard, belonging to Messrs. Hasted and Sons, and a carter's yard of Messr. Seaward Brothers. (Holmes p.298)

---

80 Holmes, p.115

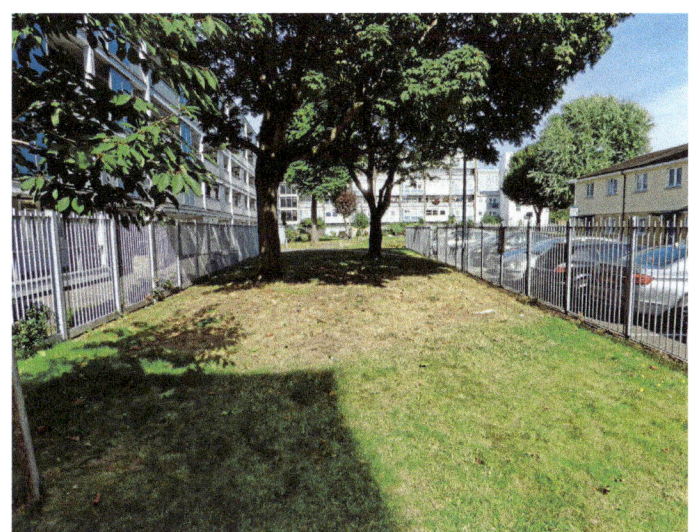

Cannon Street Road Congregational Chapel burial ground, 2016. Burials also survive under the car parking area on the right of the photo. (Photograph by A. Miles)

Walker also included, 'The burying ground … is large, and very much crowded. The fees are low; many of the Irish are buried here, and bodies are brought from very distant parishes; many of the grave stones have given way.'

There is 'a schoolroom for children at one end of the ground, built over a shed, in which are deposited pieces of broken-up coffin wood, tools, &c'. (Walker, p.173)

Sheen's Burial Ground, Nos 52–58 Commercial Road and Nos 109–153, Back Church Lane

The majority of this burial ground survives as an open area behind houses. Two pieces of archaeological work have been carried out on this ground; an evaluation carried out in 1993 defined the limits of the southern part of Sheen's burial ground on Back Church Lane, following which the design of the proposed development was changed and no impact was made on the burial ground. The second phase of work was in the northern part of the ground where 265 skeletons were excavated in 2007.[81]

Holmes describes it as, 'A private ground, immensely used. It seems to have been at one time used by the congregation of the Baptists in Little Alie Street, and was then called "Mr. Brittain's burial-ground'. After being closed for burial it was used as a cooperage, and now it is Messrs. Fairclough's yard, and full of carts and sheds, &c. A new stable was built in 1894, but the London County Council declined to prevent its erection. The size of the ground is about ½ acre'. (Homes, p.297)

Walker notes that 'SHEEN'S BURIAL GROUND, Commercial Road – This also is a private burying place. The proprietor of this ground is an undertaker. He has planted

---

81 Henderson, M, Miles, A, and Walker, D, 2013,'*He being dead yet speaketh*'. *Excavations at three post-medieval burial grounds in Tower Hamlets, East London, 2004–2008*, MOLA Monogr Ser, London

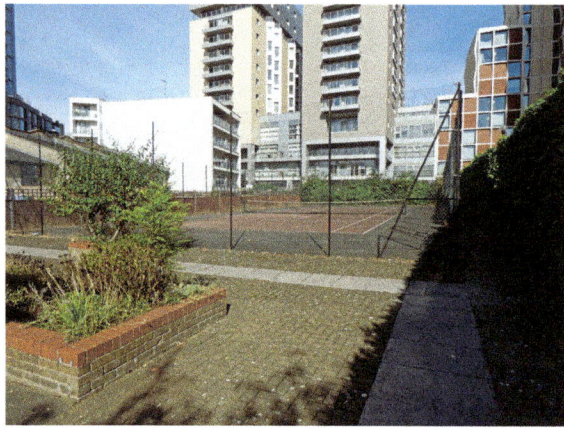

The remaining portion of Sheen's ground, Back Church Lane, today. (Photograph by A. Miles)

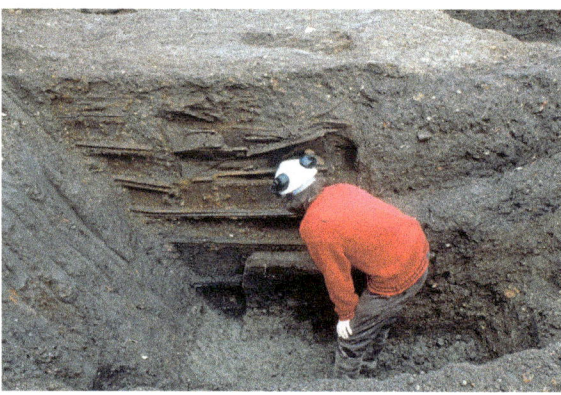

Adrian Miles cleaning stacked coffins at Sheen's burial ground. (©MOLA)

it with trees and shrubs, which are sufficiently attractive, but the ground is saturated with human putrescence'.

A dramatic incident referred to as having taken place at Mr Brittain's (or Britton) burial ground, is described in *The Times* of 23 July 1825:

ATTEMPT TO BURY MAN ALIVE

Wednesday evening, Brittain's private burial ground, in Church-row, Whitechapel, was made the scene of great uproar and confusion, which spread through the whole neighbourhood, arising from the following cause: it appeared that on Tuesday week a woman named Lucer was taken to the London hospital, where she was provided with every medical assistance; yet ... she died in a day or two afterwards, and there being marks of violence about her face, the parochial authorities deemed it necessary to institute an inquiry into the real cause of her death...The jury decided, that she had died of natural causes, and not from any violence inflicted by her husband.

The result of the inquiry did not at all satisfy the thoughtless neighbours and friends of the deceased, who persisted in stating that she had been massacred by her husband, against whom they vowed vengeance. All dissentients were Irish and Roman Catholic, whose opinions were much strengthened by the fact that he would not allow the body to be interred according to the Catholic rites, or even permit her to be 'waked,' as is customary among the Irish. This was the cause of dissatisfaction among them, and the greatest confusion that can be pictured prevailed for the last two or three days, and on Wednesday evening the burial of the wife took place.

At the hour appointed for the funeral, all the friends of the deceased assembled together, with vast numbers of their country-people, from all parts of London, not merely out of respect to the departed, but for the ostensible purpose of wreaking their vengeance on the head of the unfortunate and unoffending widower.

As the funeral procession moved on, the multitude increased, and when it reached the burial-ground, not less than from eight to ten thousand persons were present, and such was the uproar, that the Rev. Mr. Nicholl, the clergyman, was interrupted repeatedly, while reading the service, by several of the Irish calling out that the deceased did not belong to his flock. After the corpse was lowered into the grave, the general shout was to 'serve out the murdering husband'. At this signal, the husband, who was the chief mourner, was seized upon, and absolutely forced to the edge of the grave, they using the most dreadful asseverations, that he should be buried alive with his wife, whilst other [sic] were prepared with shovels to fill up the grave. The poor fellow struggled with all his might, and called for assistance, and, fortunately at this moment, a body of officers from Lambeth-street office rushed forward to save him from the dreadful sentence that awaited him, in which they succeeded with the utmost difficulty, but not till his garments were reduced to rags; and had it not been for this timely interference, they certainly would have carried their purpose into execution. The affrighted man was placed in a coach, and accompanied by officers for safety to his house.

Local Whitechapel undertaker Samuel Sheen acquired the burial ground at some point in the 1830s. A series of complaints were levelled against Sheen, which were detailed in a series of letters in *The Times* in 1846:

On Saturday, Samuel Sheen, an undertaker and proprietor of a burial ground, called 'Sheen's Cemetery', in Church-lane, Whitechapel, appeared before Mr. Ballantine, charged with using threatening and abusive language to William Jeffryes, coffin maker and furnishing undertaker

This led to a Times editorial on 23 September 1846 on the subject of burial grounds, which mentioned Sheen:

we find an undertaker of the name of Sheen possessed of a burial-ground, called 'Sheen's Cemetery', in Church-lane, Whitechapel. The existence of a place for interment in such a spot is, of itself, sufficiently objectionable. It is, however, frightful to think there is no check on the number of human remains the owner may choose to receive into his grave yard, of limited space, situated in the midst of a very densely-populated district. We do not say that this man in particular, but any man trafficking in funerals, with no motive but that of making money, is almost sure to go on crowding bodies together as closely as they can be packed, regardless alike of the health of the living of the sanctity of the dead, so long as a corpse is brought to the ground and someone is willing to pay the fee for burial. It cannot be expected that decency or humanity would operate on the minds of persons who convert a piece of land into what they call a cemetery, for the purpose of filling it with as many coffins as it will hold, at the best price the public can be induced to pay for it.

The attack continued on the 28 September:

The solemnity of the rites of the dead cannot be very seriously considered at a burial ground the gates of which are kept shut while a corpse and mourners are waiting outside, until by the perseverance of the undertaker a passage is almost forced through some private premises into the place devoted to interment. Mr Sheen's contempt for the colour of the surplice of 'our minister' may arise from a superiority to mere outward appearances, but if the 'respectable man' does not undertake to find his own official garb, it is possible that his employer's indifference to cleanliness proceeds from an eye to economy in washing bills.

Southwark

While it was not the intention of this book to cover the numerous and often interesting burial grounds south of the Thames, there are a number of burial grounds in Southwark that need comment. One in particular, the Cross Bones Ground is now one of London's most atmospheric burial grounds.

The ground, situated in Redcross Way is in the vicinity of the railway line that cuts through the area, would be totally inconspicuous were it not for many hundreds of

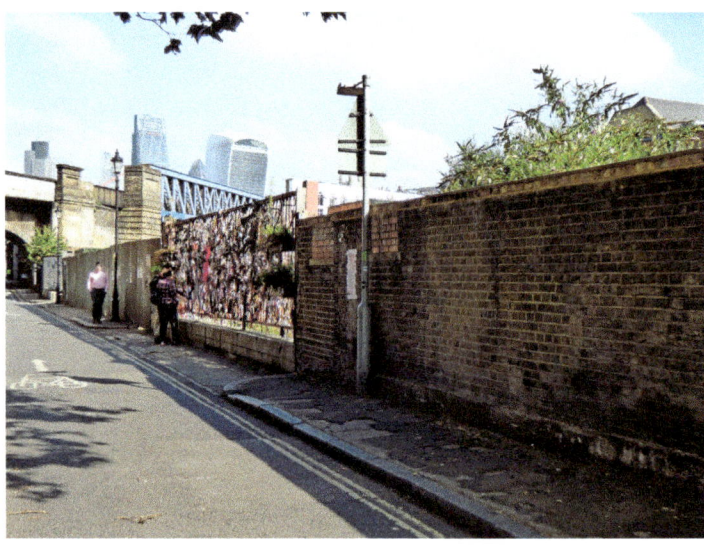

St Saviour's additional ground known as 'Cross Bones', Redcross Street (now Redcross Way), Southwark, SE1 (Photograph by A. Miles).

ribbons and notes attached to the gate beyond which the ground lies. The site belongs to Transport for London. The graveyard and the shrine have been championed by local writer John Constable, with the Friends of Crossbones, and other local individuals and companies who have campaigned for almost ten years to turn the site into a garden of remembrance. This was finally agreed by TFL in 2014 and the garden, now under the stewardship of Bankside Open Spaces Trust, is now open to the public. The Friends of Crossbones meet to hold a monthly vigil for the outcast on the 23rd of every month.

Some of the remains have been disturbed during periodic building work – once in the 1920s, and again in the 1990s when the Jubilee Line was extended. In 1896, Holmes wrote this of the small, desolate area:

> This was made, at least 250 years ago, "far from the parish church," for the interment of the low women who frequented the neighborhood. It was subsequently used as the pauper ground, and was crowded to excess. Nevertheless, two schools were built in it. The remaining piece is about 1,000 square yards. It has frequently been offered for sale as a building site, and has formed the subject for much litigation. It is made partial use of by being let for fairs, swings, &c. It was sold as building site in 1883, but, not having been used by 1884 the sale was declared (under the Disused Burial Grounds Act) null and void. (Holmes p.309)

In 1839, George Walker inevitably included the overcrowded state of this ground in his *Gatherings from Grave Yards*:

> The poor ground, called 'Cross Bones', in Red Cross Street, Union Street, Borough, also belongs to this parish. The greater portion of this ground has not been opened for some time past, in consequence of its very crowded state; the remaining part, however, is still used for interments, many of the poor Irish are buried in it. Two charity schools, one for boys and the other for girls, are built at the west end, in Union Street, the back parts of which run into this ground. On the 20th February last, a vestry meeting was holden "for the purpose of considering the propriety of re-opening the Cross Bones burying ground. "The ground had been closed about two years (*the time generally allowed for the destruction of the bodies!*) and it was moved that it be re-opened; the mover of the resolution stating, that in consequence of the aversion generally manifested to bury in what is named the "Irish corner," many bodies were taken out of the parish to be buried. *This corner, however, had been cleared, and room made for about a thousand bodies.* One gentleman argued that " if the graves had been made deeper, hundreds more corpses might have been buried there." Another admitted that it really was too bad to bury within eighteen inches of the surface, in such a crowded neighbourhood; and it was even hinted that "*the clearing,*" viz. the digging up and the removal *of the decayed fragments of flesh and bones, with the pieces of coffin, &c. would be the best course, were it not for the additional expense.*"

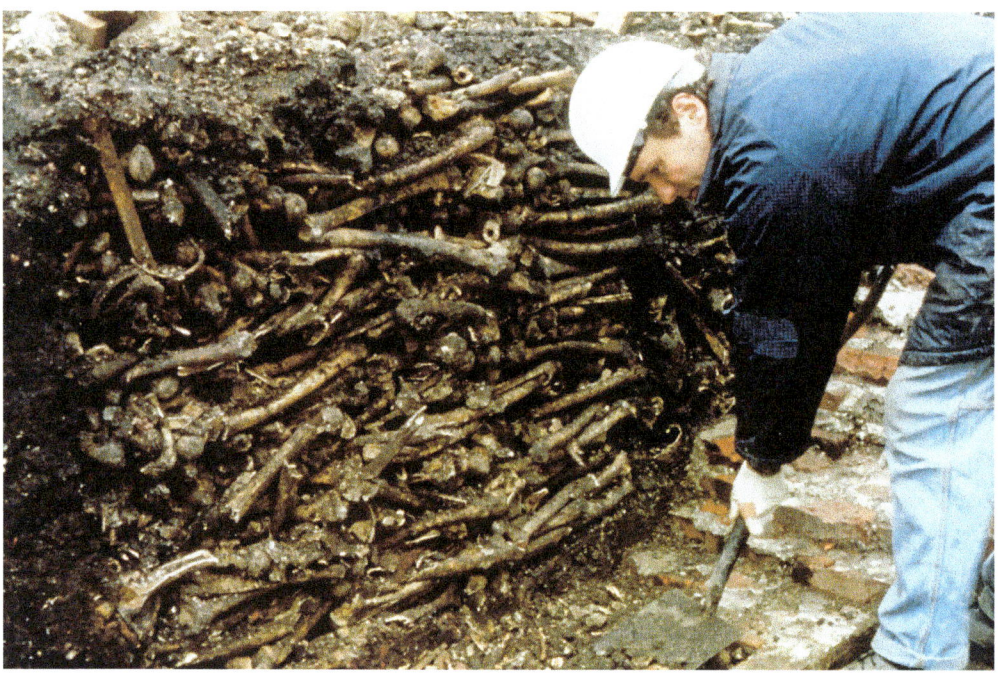

Layers of bones at the Cross Bones burial ground. (From MOLAS publication *The Cross Bones Burial Ground*, Fig 3, p.4)

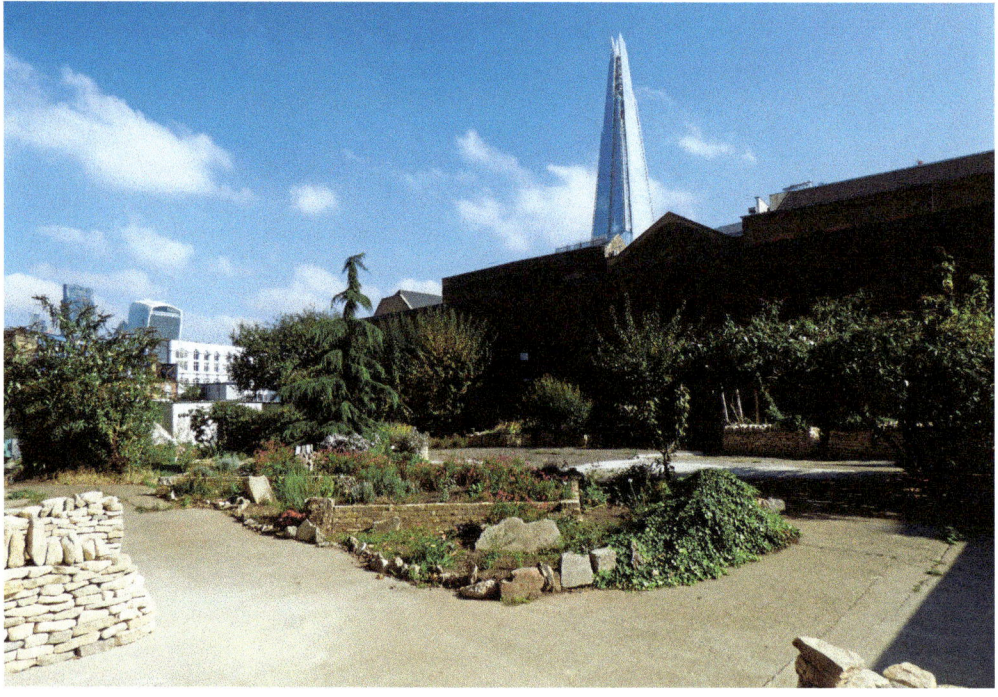

The Crossbones memorial garden. (Photograph by A. Miles)

> The *fund* of the vestry and the *health* of the living were here placed in opposite scales: the former had its preponderance.[82]

A note to the vestry in 1832 shows that all was not well with the burial ground:

> having viewed with much attention the Cross Bones Burial Ground, find it so very full of coffins that it is necessary to bury within two feet of the surface which we consider, especially under the alarming disease now raging, to be very improper. We also find on a partial opening of the ground that the effluvium is so very offensive that we fear the consequences may be very injurious to the surrounding neighbourhood. We therefore are of the opinion under such circumstances and the expectation of close warm weather that the Ground ought to be immediately closed.[83]

However, it remained open. A further attempt to have the ground closed took place in August 1845 when Mariane Gwilt, who lived in the immediate vicinity at the school house in Union Street, complained to the Board of Health, painting a graphic and unsettling picture of the state of the ground:

> From the windows of the room called the School room we have all this sickly Summer almost daily witnessed the most distressing sights; our remonstrances are vain – in the bone house with its open grating which is not more than *eight* or *ten* yards from five of our windows we have during these last fatal six weeks had sometimes as many as from three to nine bodies lying in their shells (coffins) at a time for days (as many as ten days) in the aforesaid Bone house close under our windows, - One of these shells contained the body of a woman who was brought here supposed dead from Cholera, but actually broke a blood vessel, trying to get out, whilst being carried along she not being dead then - The saw dust and shavings saturated with blood which washed out the shell when the body was transferred into the permanent Coffin was spread under our windows and is there now although this occurred three weeks ago. On another occasion three or four weeks since the body of a man who had drowned himself at Blackfriars Bridge was brought down here and allowed to lie in its shell ten days when the body was washed with a mop and pailsful of water and the shell again washed out and all the filthy liquid and shavings and grass thrown under our windows his clothes lie there at this time I am writing and whilst he lay'd there the bodies of two children who had died of the Cholera was left in this dead house the chief of the time.....Our kitchen on the ground floor with the School room over it forms the wing which looks into this burial ground – the earth of which comes at least four feet above the level of the said kitchen floor owing to the number of burials which take place and it is now rendered very damp and unhealthy[84]

---

82 Walker, pp.177-178
83 *The Cross Bones Burial Ground*, p.9
84 Extract from *The Cross Bones Burial Ground*, p.12 (MoLAS)

The Board of Health denied Gwilt's complaints, but in November 1852 a further complaint was received which began: 'We the ... Inhabitants of the High Street of Union Street and Red Cross Street in the Borough of Southwark, whose dwellings are near unto or adjoining the Cross Bones Grave Yard....'

It continues to state that they had hoped the ground would have been closed, but to their disappointment it still operated.

> This small plot of ground containing under 12000 superficial feet for more than 300 years has been made to receive a very large proportion of the paupers and all the parochial poor to a very enormous extent, this is owing to the cheapness compared with the burial expenses in the Grave Yard surrounding the Parish Church....Now it has been proved by Parishioners and by the parish documents and never disputed to this day that the number of bodies deposited in this patch of ground taking the aggregate of any seven years during this half century past placing them side by side upon their feet and two deep over each other and packed without coffins the allotments would not contain them. Therefore, in consequences of this want of room the Gravedigger is daily seen with a long steel pointed Iron Rod sticking the ground here and there spearing the top coffins, until some wood gives way, whereupon the whole of the contents, whereupon the whole of the contents, however manifold the coffins may be 'sometimes many' in that particular Grave are turned out and remain several days above ground to the scandal of all Christian men. When each of these exhumations have taken place there have been seen and repeatedly counted in different lots of such human remains 'a number of skulls too numerous lying like half devoured Turnips about a Sheepfold and cared for as little'[85]

The response to the above letter was that the graveyard was finally closed in 1853, on the grounds that it was 'completely overcharged with dead' and that 'further burials' would be 'inconsistent with a due regard for the public health and public decency'. In 1883, it was sold as a building site, prompting Lord Brabazon to write to *The Times*: '... with a view to save this ground from such desecration, and to retain it as an open space for the use and enjoyment of the people'. (10 November 1883)

In 1928 some bones were disturbed during building work. A newspaper cutting of the time observes that,

> During the early part of the year, whilst a site at the Corner of Red Cross and Union Streets was being excavated, a number of human remains was unearthed, skulls and limb bones predominating. They were found six feet below the surface, and descended to a depth of ten feet. These bones were of considerable antiquity and were those of persons from 25 years of age and upwards. They were carefully placed and had undoubtedly been moved here at some former period from another part of

---

[85] Letter taken from *The Cross Bones Burial Ground*, P.15

the site and re-interred in this excavation and covered over at the time with a layer of lime concrete several inches in thickness, in which some of the skulls and bones were embedded wherever excavations were made bones were found, and the quantity actually brought to the surface would represent about forty persons, and a greater number still remain.[86]

The forty skeletons were placed in coffins and reburied at Brookwood Cemetery. The following year, the sale was declared null and void under the Disused Burial Grounds Act (1884). Subsequent attempts to develop the site were fiercely resisted by local people. The land was briefly used as a fairground.

In 1993, as part of the Jubilee Line Extension project, London Underground built an electricity substation to supply power for the line. The Museum of London Archaeologists conducted a partial excavation of the site down to the level required for a slab foundation, removing 148 skeletons. These probably represented less than 1 per cent of the total number of burials that took place at this site. It was determined by the project engineers that more substantial foundations were required than originally planned, so further exhumation was carried out within the same footprint, with no archaeological oversight. However, there are still several thousand burials within the site. The fence line of the new garden represents the northern limit of the burial ground. Some skeletons from the site were exhibited at the museum's 1998 London Bodies exhibition, the Wellcome Institute's Skeletons: London's Buried Bones exhibition, in 2008 and have been subject to study in the BBC's *History Cold Case* series.

Ewer Street Chapel and Burial Ground, SE1

There is little to see of this burial ground situated in Ewer Street, around 500 yards from where it joins Union Street. It lies immediately alongside the Charing Cross Railway. The blue gate on the right of the illustration marks the entrance to the site. The atmosphere is Dickensian. Walker says this of the ground:

EWER STREET CHAPEL AND BURYING GROUND, at the bottom of Union Street, Borough. The burying ground appears to have been raised nearly six feet from the original surface, and is literally surcharged with dead; it is now closed, and presents a very repulsive aspect. It might be instructive to know the number of bodies here inhumed; perhaps, - but dead men tell no tales, - the exhumed might present a formidable array. The vicinity is disgustingly dirty.[87]

Some bodies were removed in around 1861 when the Charing Cross Railway was built, though judging by recent finds many bodies were left in situ. The date of discovery of the bodies mentioned below was actually June 1987. The SE1 community website comments,

---

86 ibid. p.19
87 Walker, p 179

this is the site of an unmarked graveyard, as discovered in about 1990 by some workmen who were renewing the concrete floor under two of the railway arches when they came across about a skull. Suspecting foul play, the police were called in. The police called in a pathologist. He called in an archaeologist... about 200 skeletons were eventually unearthed ...the bones were reburied elsewhere (but only two of the arches were excavated). It appears that when the viaduct was built the contractors came across the graveyard, said nothing and moved the graves which were in the way of the piers, resulting in a lot of the bodies being reburied standing up and bones just jumbled up together very close to the surface.[88]

Additional Ground for St Saviour's, called the College Yard or St Saviour's Almshouse Burial Ground, Park Street, SE1

This ground came into use around 1730, and was purchased in 1860 by Charing Cross Railway when railway arches were built over the ground. Human remains were uncovered and moved to both Brookwood Cemetery, near Woking, and Nunhead Cemetery. The rest of the ground was used as a builder's yard and is now a car park for The Hop Exchange. In 1896, Holmes says that the ground 'existed before 1732. Size, ¼ acre. The London, Brighton and South Coast Railway goes over it on arches, and it is now the store yard of Messrs. Stone and Humphries, builders. Most of it is roofed

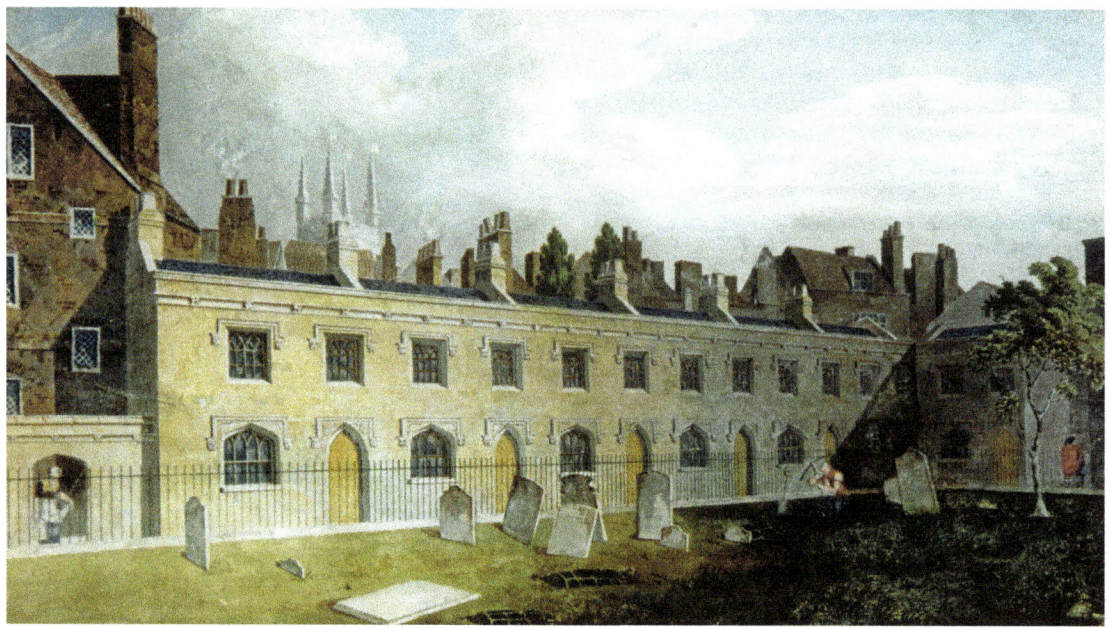

The College Burial Ground during the first half of the nineteenth century. (London Met. Archives, taken from *Cross Bones* Book Ill, p.7).

---

88 From SE1 community website forum 2002

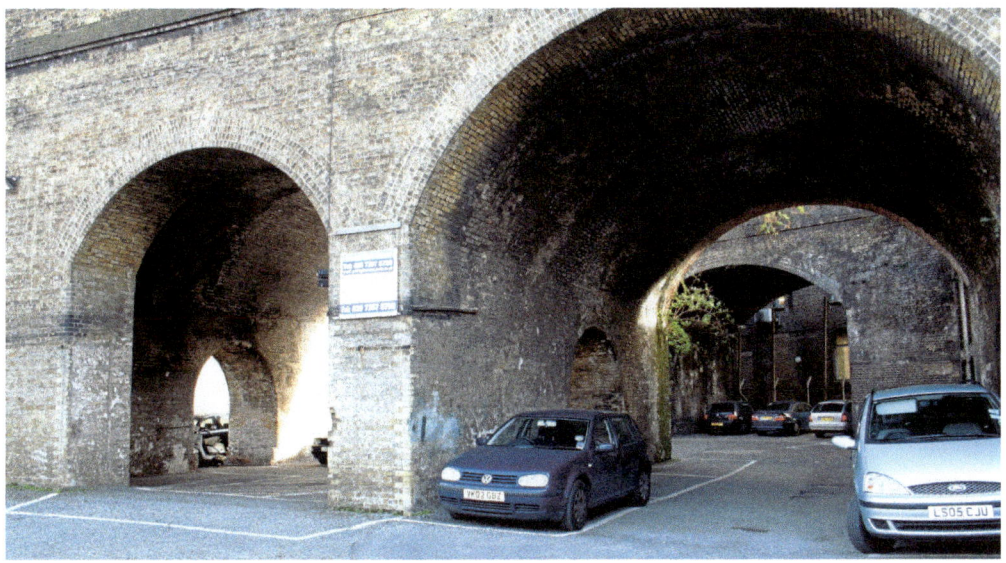

College Yard or St Saviour's Almshouse Burial Ground, Park Street. The ground was destroyed by the railway in 1860. (Photograph by R. Bard)

in but it is not actually covered with buildings'. (Holmes, p.309). A further portion of the ground was excavated in 2009–10 when new viaduct foundations were required as part of the Thameslink project; 332 individual skeletons were excavated by MOLA.

Friends' Burial Ground, Worcester Street (Now O'Meara Street), SE1
The car park next to the Charing Cross railway arch is the site of a Quaker burial ground, which was in use by 1666. There was a Friends Meeting House to the south of O'Meara Street that had its own burial ground. This was built in 1674. The Worcester Street ground was full by 1733, and the ground level was raised to allow more burials. The ground closed in 1794, and in 1860 the land was compulsorily purchased by the Metropolitan Board of Works to build Southwark Street. The ground was destroyed when the London Bridge–Charing Cross Railway was constructed in 1860. The Friends supervised the clearing of the ground in 1860. A report of the exhumations from 1860 states that, 'with the exception of lead coffins in various states of preservation, the remains were found to have become reduced to skeletons; and although there was a considerable amount of loose coffin wood…no bodies were found nearer the surface than seven feet, showing the care Friends had taken not to overcrowd the ground … [the remains] were all removed (by hearse) at various times to the burial-ground at Long Lane, Bermondsey….'[89] The report goes on to observe that 956 remains were

---

[89] 'The O'Meara Street grouting shaft excavation report', Chapter 8, pp49-51 taken from the Museum of London publication, The Cross Bones Burial Ground, Redcross Way, Southwark, London, Molas Monograph 3).

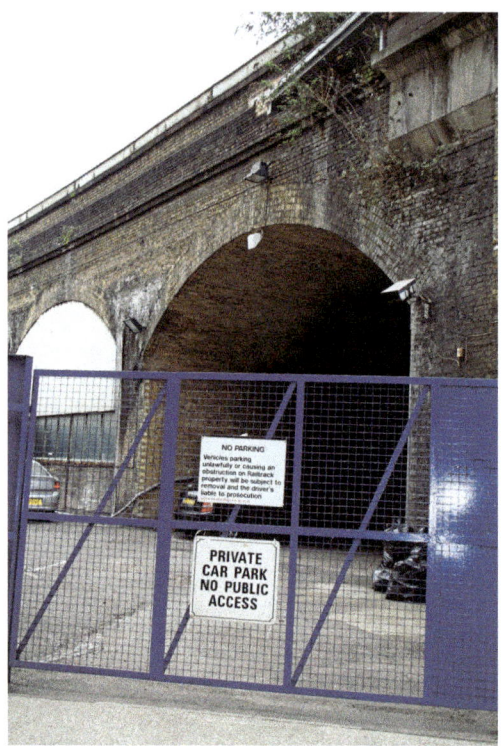

The site of a Quaker burial ground in use from at least 1666. The construction of the railway destroyed the ground. Nine bodies were found on this site during work on the Jubilee Line Extension in October 1994. (Photograph by R. Bard)

exhumed. A number of lead coffins were found, and then opened to see the state of preservation of the corpses – the conclusion being that, in general, burial in lead did little to halt decomposition. The exhumations by no means included the total number interred. In October 1994, nine bodies were found here during work on the Jubilee Line Extension project. It is now a scruffy car park on the corner of Southwark Street and O'Meara Street. (Site code OMS94, London Archaeologist Round-up 1994.)

New Bunhill Fields Burial Ground, Deverell Street, Southwark

This site is situated within the playground of the Globe Academy on Harper Road. A part of it was excavated in 2008 during the construction of a new building. The burial ground was established in around 1821 as a commercial Nonconformist ground; as many as 33,000 burials may have taken place before its closure in 1853. 827 burials were recorded archaeologically by MOLA.[90]

A chapel fronting onto Deverell Street was present on the site from 1826, which sat over a semi-sunken burial vault. The first proprietor of the burial ground was Joseph Hoole, an undertaker of Kent Road. He appears to have gone into partnership with Thomas Martin by 1826, and it is Martin's name that is mainly associated with the ground.

---

90 Miles, A, with Connell, B, 2012 New Bunhill Fields burial ground, Southwark: Excavations at Globe Academy, 2008 MOLA Archaeology studies series 24, London

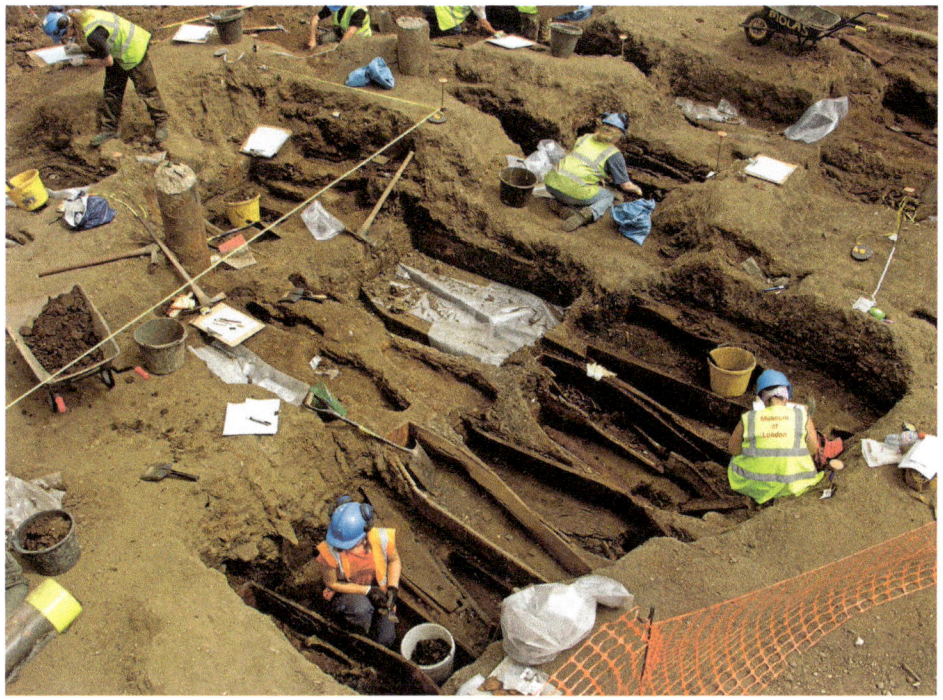

Excavations at New Bunhill Fields, Southwark, showing how tightly packed the coffins were. (©MOLA)

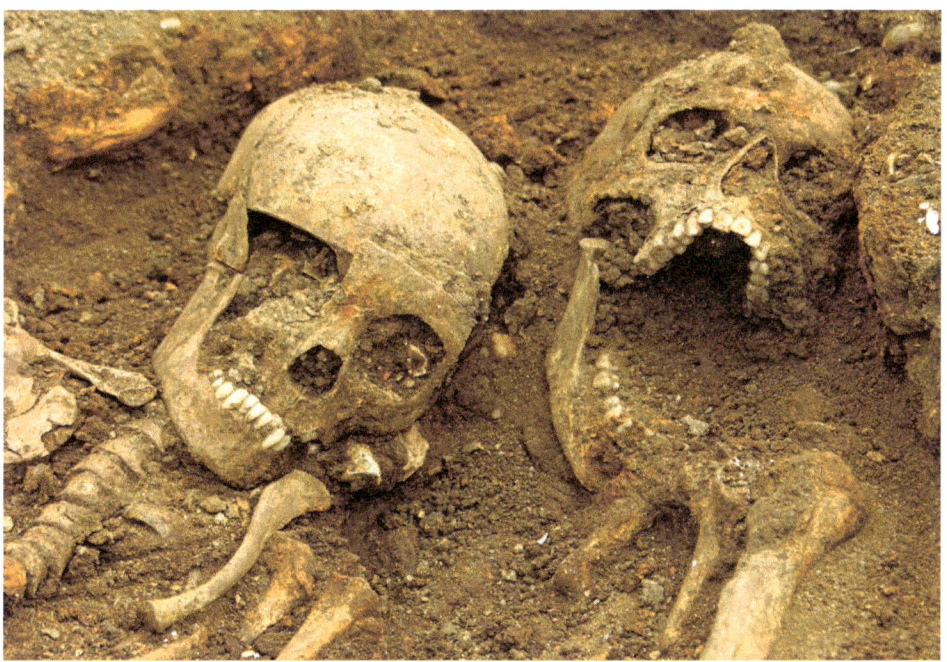

Autopsied skull on the left from New Bunhill Fields, Southwark. (©MOLA)

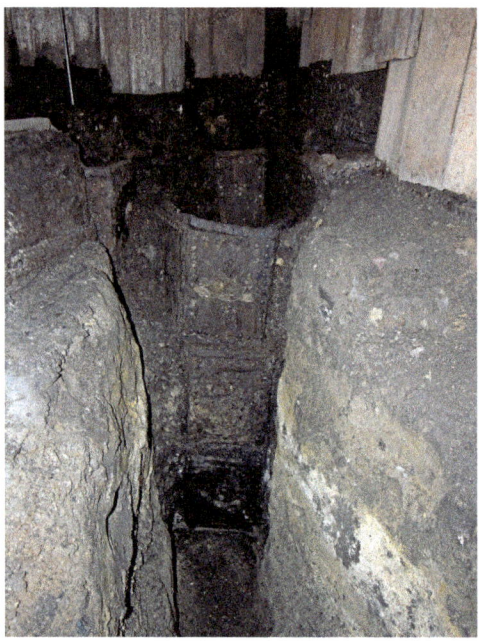

Coffins stacked in a single grave, from New Bunhill Fields, Southwark. (©MOLA)

Walker mentions both the burial ground and the vault below the chapel in *Gatherings from Graveyards*:

NEW BUNHILL FIELDS - This burying ground is situated in the New Kent Road; it is a private speculation, and belongs to Mr. Martin, an undertaker.

It has many attractions for survivors; the fees are low, the grounds are walled round and well watched, and the superintendent of the place resides upon the spot. At the entrance of the ground a chapel has been erected; it belongs to the Wesleyan connexion; under this chapel, arched with strong brick-work, is a spacious vault, containing about eighteen hundred coffins. There are not more, I believe, than twelve bodies placed in lead out of the entire number. Iron gratings are placed on each side of the vault, and its entrance is by steps, through rather an extensive doorway. It appears that the original proprietor of the place was named Hoole. Two coffins, one containing his remains, and the other, stated to contain the remains of his daughter, are placed in the bottom of the vault, at the upper end, on the left hand side of it, enclosed with iron railings.

The other coffins are placed in rows, one above the other; some of them distinguished by small plates, placed upon the end or sides of the coffins, having particular inscriptions...

A strong ammoniacal odour pervades this vault; it is not so offensive as that which I have experienced in most other depositories of this description; this I attribute, to the constant transmission of the noxious vapours, (through open iron gratings) to the circumambient atmosphere. The burial ground and vault, it appears, have been employed, for the purposes of interment, about eighteen years, during which, not less than ten thousand bodies have been inhumed and deposited, within this 'narrow spot of earth,' and the vault connected with it. Yet, around this tainted atmosphere, many houses are erected and boards are placed offering ground to be let upon building leases! (Walker 181–2)

Walker again wrote about New Bunhill Fields in 1847 in the second of a series of lectures delivered at the Mechanics Institution:

Haycock worked as gravedigger in that ground during 10 years. He says the place had been open during 18 years and had received nearly 21,000 bodies by 1842. 21,000 bodies in an acre of ground and in the vault of the chapel where the worshippers assembled.

Haycock is asked for an explanation of the mode by which 20,000 coffins had been placed in an acre of ground. He says 'we dig 10 foot and if we can get 12 foot we do, and then we pile them one upon the other as many as the grave will hold, perhaps 6 or 8 or 9 in it; then when that is full, we dig another grave close by the side of it and put another nine or ten therein; that they were piled one on another, just as if you were piling up bricks'. He says the smell was 'dreadful, beyond all smells', that he himself, raised the ground all over the place about 6 inches; that the burial service was read over the graves by a patten-maker, who lived close by. He had £20 a year ... so it suits him well.

Haycock stated that at one time bodies were stacked in the vault at the rate of £1 each for 6 month ... what becomes of them after the expiration of the 6 months tenancy he does not say.

The ways of the wicked, however, are not always prosperous, and a just providence sometimes demonstrates his wrath by nature of the punishment which overtakes the guilty. This same Hoole ... fell victim to his beastly occupation. A report appeared in a morning paper that 'his vault was over the shoes in human corruption'. The fear of the press inspired him with a sudden desire to set his house in order; he came in from the country, worked in his shirt-sleeves at the piles of decaying matter heaped up in the vault, went home ill, and together with his 'head man' died in a few days. So may the unrighteous perish!

Haycock, who died of consumption about 9 months ago, told me some years since that 'the stench in digging graves in that ground was horrible'; that he had frequently scrambled out of the hole he was making, - that his eyes struck fire, - his brain seemed in a whirl, and that he vomited large quantities of blood.

Haycock, although an exceedingly strong man when he commenced grave digging, offers another evidence, amongst too many others, of the power of emanations from the dead over the health of the living. I knew him and attended him occasionally, during many years. I saw him droop, die inch by inch; and although the disease was held under control during a short period, his life paid the forfeit. (Walker 1849)

The Era newspaper reported, on 2 September 1849, how Mr Cookson, an inhabitant of the New Kent Road, applied for a magistrate's advice:

…with respect to an over-crowded burial-ground, situated in Deverell-street, and which was calculated to diffuse sickness over the neighbourhood. He said that the ground in question had been in existence for a great number of years as a burial-place, and that owing to the immense number of bodies which were deposited therein, many of the coffins were so near the surface, and scarcely covered with earth, that the effluvia arising therefrom was of the most sickening and dangerous description. That every day from fifteen to twenty interments took place, and on Sundays double the number, and although the ground was so full of human remains, still the parties interested contrived to crowd the place still more, until it had become a perfect nuisance, and that one of the worst description, in a crowded neighbourhood.

Three years later, *The Daily News* for 12 October 1852 reported on the findings of a parliamentary committee:

The nuisance here is unabated; for I was assured by the respectable mistress of an inn, at a good many yards distance, that amidst all their lemons and liqueurs and strong-smelling spirits, the stench from this burial-ground was at times very bad, and very sickening indeed. It was no injury to her pocket, for customers drank to drown it; but it was very bad. A man connected with the ground told me that everything had been remedied 'as was complained about;' and there had been an addition to the extent of the ground, which was 'as sweet as a carrot.' The sole addition to be seen is a small strip in one corner, marked as if for vaults, where vaults could hardly be, and containing no graves, but two tasteless flower-beds, and two cucumber frames; one on a heap of stable manure.

4. Disused and Hidden Jewish Burial Grounds

Holmes refers to a number of areas which were used for the burial of Jews. Prior to the year 1177, there was only one place that Jews were allowed to be buried. Holmes tells us that,

> It was known as the Jews' Garden and was outside the wall of London by Cripplegate, several acres being devoted to the purpose – a neighbourhood subsequently known by the name of Leyrestowe. When other burial-places were permitted, this ground was built upon, but the remembrance of it still lives in the name of one street in the district, Jewin Street, reminding us of the time of the bitter persecutions which the Jews suffered....[91]

Jewin Street, or 'Jewen' on the Rocque map, is situated just to the east of the Barbican, off of Aldersgate Street. Holmes observes that its very size and position made it inevitable that it would disappear under the coming streets as London grew and the land became more and more valuable. A number of Jewish cemeteries are commented on.

Jewish Burial Ground, Fulham Road

This burial fronts onto the Fulham Road and is totally anonymous to the passer-by. Behind a black locked door lies a cemetery, overlooked by the nearby flats, but otherwise not visible from the street.

Of this former mulberry orchard, Holmes (1896) says that it was half an acre and 'belongs to the Western Synagogue, St. Alban's Place, S. W., and was first used in 1813. It is closed to the public except between 11 and 4 on Sundays'.[92] Without knowledge of its location, finding this ground would be bordering on the impossible, unless one lives in one of the flats overlooking this area of quiet seclusion in the heart of the busy Fulham Road.

---

[91] Holmes, p.155
[92] Holmes, p.283

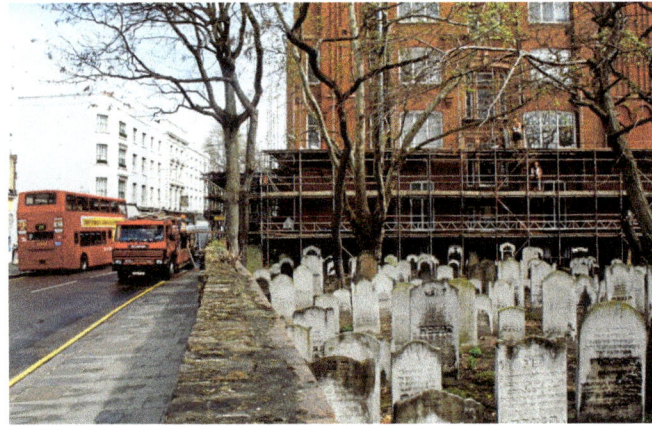

This disused cemetery was first used in 1813 and lies hidden behind a wall on the Fulham Road. (Photograph by R. Bard)

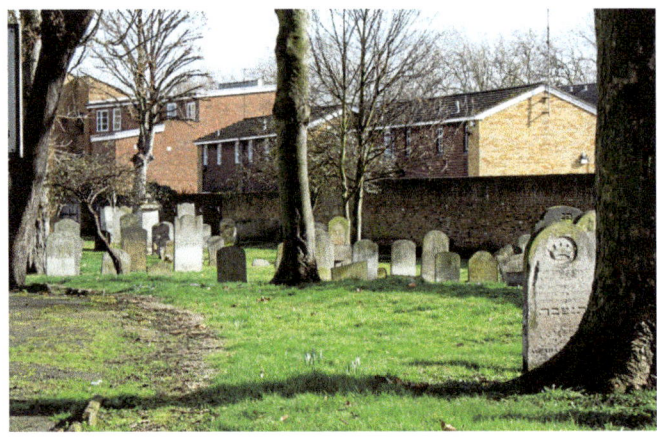

The southern end of the ground is the most atmospheric. (Photograph by R. Bard)

Jewish Burial Ground, Lauriston Road formerly Grove Street Hackney, E9

The cemetery is a prominent feature in Lauriston Road. The ground came into use by 1788 and was used until the closure of the Hambro Synagogue in London in 1892. The cemetery is closed and is still recognizable from Holmes' brief 1896 description: '2¼ acres. This belongs to the United Synagogue, and was purchased in 1788. It is closed and full of erect tombstones, and has some trees and flower-beds near the entrance'.

The Hoxton Cemetery was originally formed for use by the Hambro Synagogue in Fenchurch Street, and first came into use around 1700.

Alderney Road Cemetery, Stepney, London, E1

There is a little-known cemetery near to London's Stepney Green Underground Station. It is the first Ashkenasi burial ground in England after the resettlement in 1656. Benjamin Levy, acting from the highest motives of disinterest because his own burial rights were secure, bought from Capt. Nathaniel Owen a plot of land contiguous with

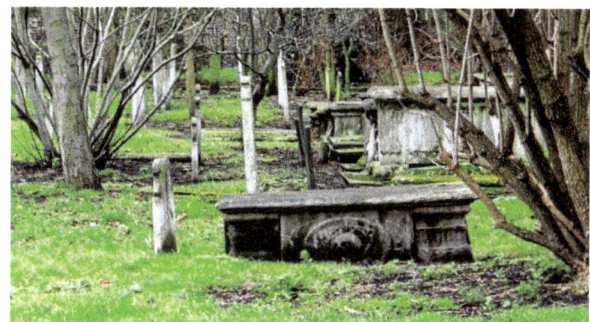

This tomb is unusual in a Jewish cemetery in that it has a prominent skull motif. (Photograph by R. Bard)

Sephardi Cemetery in Mile End on 2 February 1696 (Old Style) or 2 February 1697 (New Style) on a lease for 999 years, at a peppercorn rent of £190.

By the middle of the eighteenth century it was necessary to purchase a further plot immediately adjacent. This was in Three Colt Yard.

The ground opened in around 1697 and was extended in 1749. It closed in 1852. It is situated close to Stepney Green Station and the site of the People's Palace. It is described as being in Three Colt Yard. The Rocque map shows that Three Colt Yard is some hundred yards to the west of the Mile End Road Cemetery, which is shown on the map as the 'Jews Old Burying Ground'. Holmes, in 1896, describes the latter as being 'nearly five acres in extent and still in use, just beyond the People's Palace'.[93]

It would seem that this cemetery was guarded energetically against the 'Resurrection Men':

> A feature of the Cemetery in the old days was a sort of wheeled sentry-box, which was moved about the ground and from which new graves were watched for some nights after a burial had taken place, as a precaution against the activities of the so-called 'Resurrection men' who supplied Medical Schools with corpses for dissection. Members of the Congregation, in pairs and armed with blunderbusses, took turns to perform this cold and rather gruesome duty, and in the records of the Synagogue there are preserved rosters of the roll of duty 'for the guarding of the House of Life'.[94]

Brady Street (Bethnal Green), formerly North Street, E1

Brady Street Cemetery is not easy to find. It is located behind a wall protected by broken glass a little way past Mocatto House on the left-hand side, when approached from the Brady Street junction with the Whitechapel Road. There is an area of wall that can be peered over, but an appointment needs to be made with the United Synagogue burial authority to be allowed entry. The cemetery, which opened in 1761, is unusual because a raised area in the centre of the cemetery was created for 'foreigners'. A 4-foot-deep

---

93 Holmes, p.159
94 F:\Alderney Road Monumental Inscriptions.htm

layer of soil was added so that multiple layers of burials could take place. Coffins had to be separated by at least 6 feet. The headstones in this area lie back to back. Holmes, writing in 1896, says this of the now disused cemetery:

> ...there are walls running through it, and the southern half is higher than the northern half, having quite a hilly appearance. The following is the explanation. This half of the ground was originally allotted to 'strangers,' Jews who belonged to no special congregation. About thirty years after it was full, a layer of earth, 4 feet in depth, was added to the ground, and it was used over again. As the coffins were again placed 6 feet from the surface, there still remained 4 feet of earth between them and the old ones beneath. As a result of this curious and interesting arrangement, there may be seen, in several cases, two gravestones standing up back to back, which represent the two graves below them. [95]

Probably three of the most interesting tombs are those of Nathan Mayer Rothschild, his wife Hannah, and Nathaniel Mayer Rothschild, the 3rd Baron Rothschild. Nathan

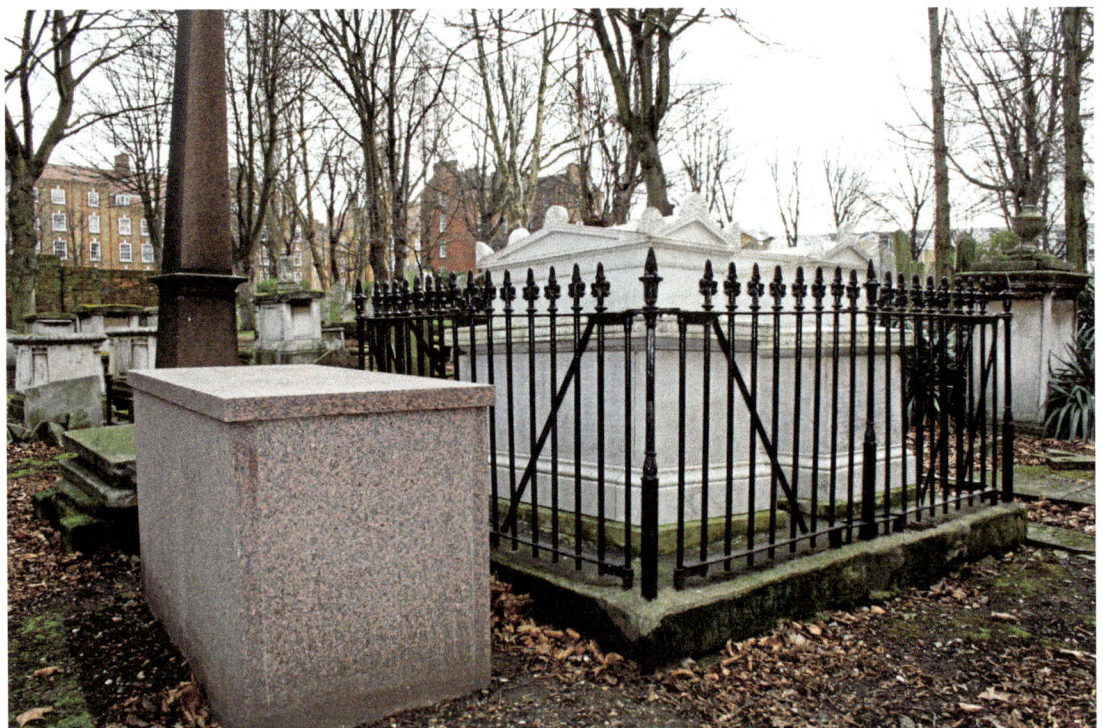

The two Rothschild tombs mentioned by Holmes. The third tomb on the left is that of Nathaniel Victor Mayer Rothschild, the 3rd Baron, who was buried here in 1990 to prevent the cemetery from being used for development until at least 2090. (Photograph by R. Bard)

---

95 Holmes, p.157

died in 1836, and Nathaniel in 1990. He decided he would be buried next to his ancestors to prevent the local council from placing a compulsory purchase order on the site. The burial meant that the burial ground was safe for another 100 years.

In 1665 the great plague devastated London and the Jewish community suffered heavily. It is known that at least 6 victims of the plague were buried in what was then the new cemetery in Mile End Road. Another cemetery was opened in 1791. In 1811 observant German Jewish immigrants dissatisfied with the Great Synagogue in Dukes Place formed the 'New Synagogue' in Leadenhall Street in the City. In that time it was incumbent upon every synagogue to provide its own burial grounds and the 'New' leased this place at 12 guineas per annum as a cemetery. So this cemetery is the third oldest and largest for its time. (It must be remembered that United Synagogues comprising the 'Great', the 'New' and Hambro was only formed in 1870 and shared burial grounds). By 1840 little space was left here and to extend the number of graves available it was decided to put a four-foot layer of earth on top of the centre ground and bury on top. This has resulted in a large flat-topped mound in the centre with headstones back to back - the one stone for the grave below and the one for the one above. The cemetery closed in 1858 except for reserved graves.[96]

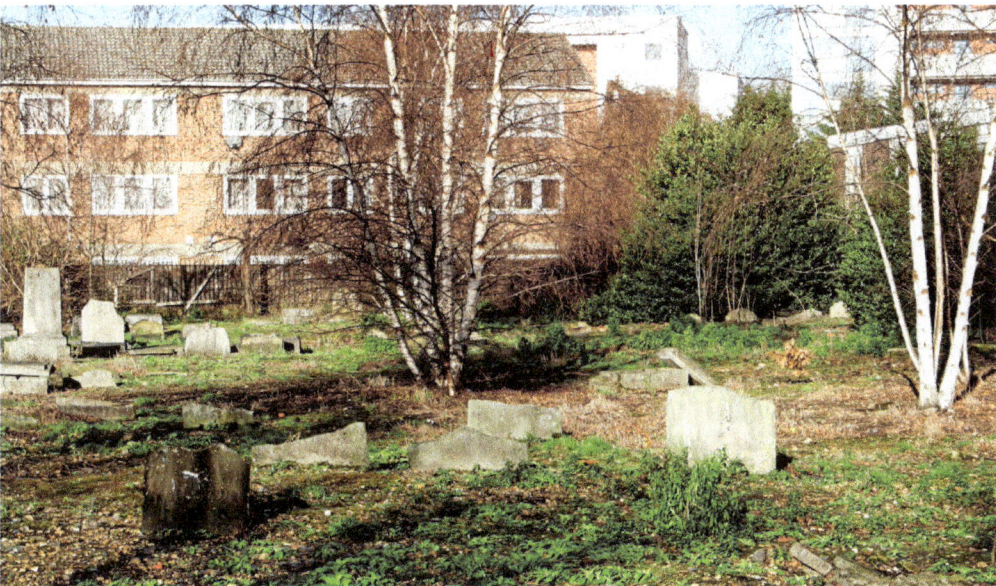

Brady Street Cemetery showing the raised centre section for double burials where 'foreigners' or non-local Jews were buried. (Photograph by R. Bard)

---

96 See article on Brady Street cemetery http://www.ibiblio.org/yiddish/Places/London/london.htm

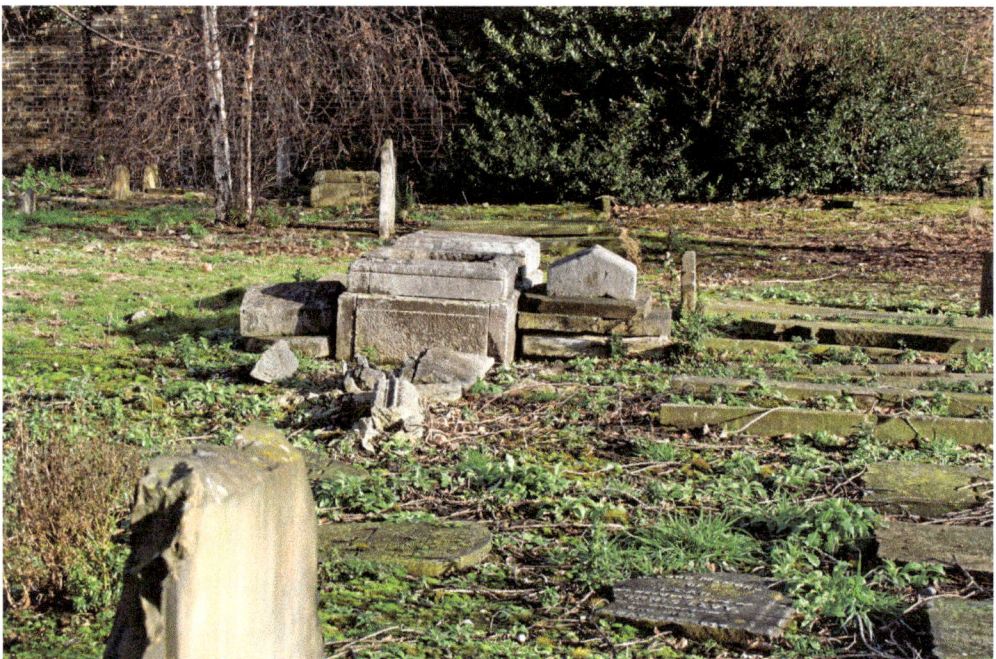

First used in 1811, by 1884 it had fallen into a state of disrepair and by 1895 it was practically filled up. The cemetery is atmospheric but crumbling and neglected. (Photograph by R. Bard)

Bancroft Road, Tower Hamlets, E1

The Bancroft Road Jewish Cemetery came into use in 1811, and by 1884 the cemetery was observed by the *Jewish Chronicle* newspaper to be in a state of disrepair. This cemetery is described in 1896 by Holmes as 'another dreary place, which, although in so crowded a district, is still in use'. She comments that when she visited prior to 1896, there was room for four more graves. Today, the cemetery is still there. It is situated in Bancroft Road, which is largely residential. It has been described as desolate and, as observed by Holmes over a century ago, lies in the heart of a crowded district – more than dreary, the cemetery is badly vandalised with very few gravestones still standing. Over a century later little has changed. The cemetery is in a terrible state of decay.

The cemetery was bombed during the Second World War and evidence of the damage can still be seen. Many of the tombstones lie flat with jagged scars.

Old Velho Sephardi Cemetery, behind Albert Stern House at No. 253 Mile End Road

This cemetery is extremely difficult to locate. It is situated directly behind No. 253 Mile End Road. The immediate surroundings are a tiny remnant of Victorian London. The entrance is by way of a small archway, and entrance to the graveyard itself is by prior appointment. Some careful peeking over a wall, bearing in mind the various health and safety aspects, will allow a panoramic view of the cemetery, which essentially remains the same as in Mrs Holmes' 1896 photograph.

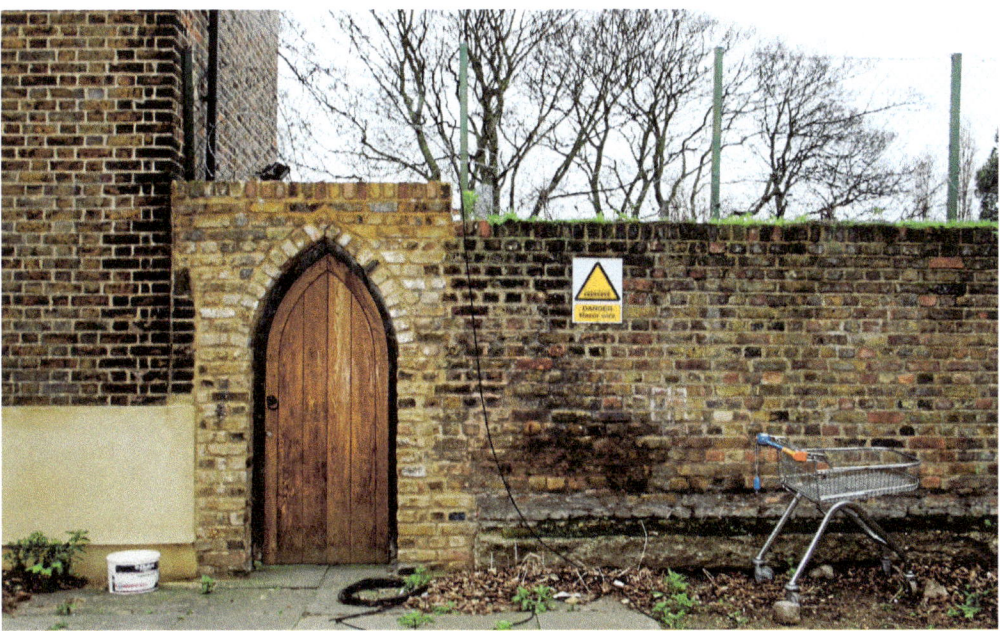

The cemetery is locked. An appointment is needed for entry. It can be seen by peering over the wall, but there are a number of associated hazards. (Photograph by R. Bard)

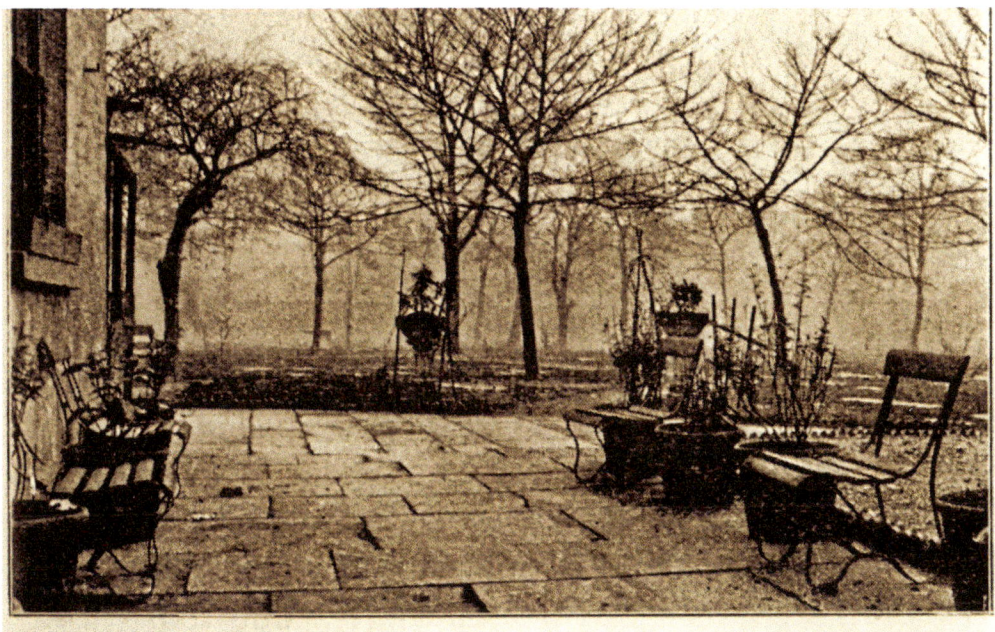

The cemetery from an 1896 photograph, showing the Beth Holim Hospital to the left. Albert Stern House was built in its place in 1913. (Photograph by Holmes, 1896)

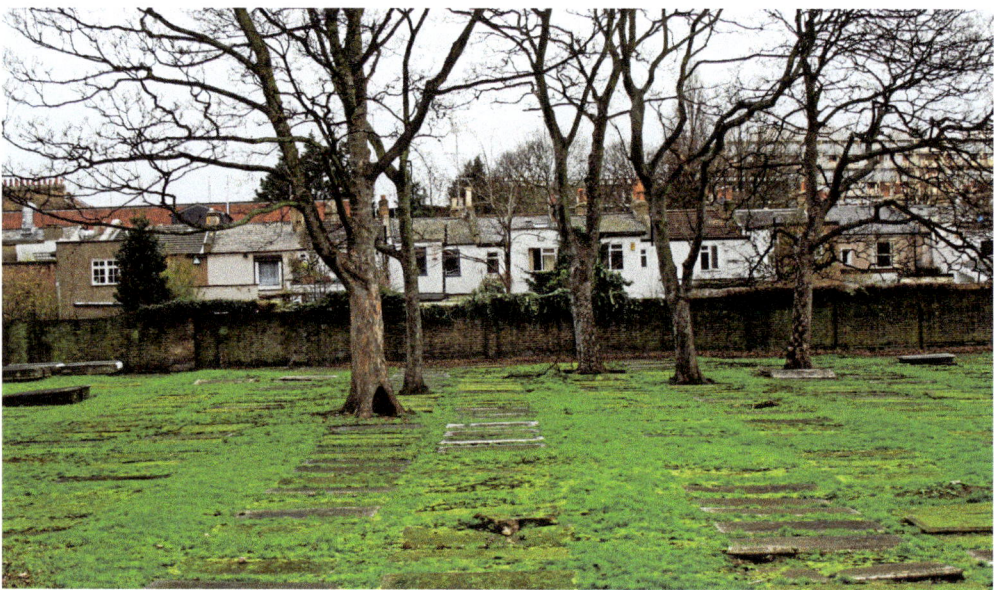

The old cemetery. Albert Stern House is situated to the left. (Photograph by R. Bard)

There is a plaque on the front Albert Stern House which states that

Behind this building lies the first cemetery of the Spanish and Portuguese Jews who fled from the persecutions of the Spanish and Portuguese Inquisition to find religious toleration and freedom in this realm. They founded in the City of London in 1650 the congregation called Shaar HaShamayim-The Gate of Heaven-which is still in existence. It was the first professing Jewish community in the British Isles established in Modern times and formed the origin of the present Jewish community of Britain as a whole. For admission to the old cemetery of the Spanish and Portuguese Jews apply to: The Secretary, Spanish & Portuguese Jews congregation … etc.

Novo Beth Chaim Sephardi Cemetery, Queen Mary College Campus, Mile End Road, E1

This cemetery was opened in 1725 and closed in the 1920s. Viewing this cemetery requires entry to the Queen Mary's college campus, which is situated on the Mile End Road. The cemetery is situated near the Faculty of Arts building and is easily accessible. It lies on the eastern side and provides a sobering contrast with the vibrant daily campus life that goes on around it, without scarcely a glance or thought. The cemetery was partly built over when the campus expanded in the 1970s with the remains of some 7,500 deceased being exhumed. Around 2,000 graves remain. [97]

---

[97] I am grateful to Philip Walker and his marvellous website for much of the information relating to the Jewish cemeteries.

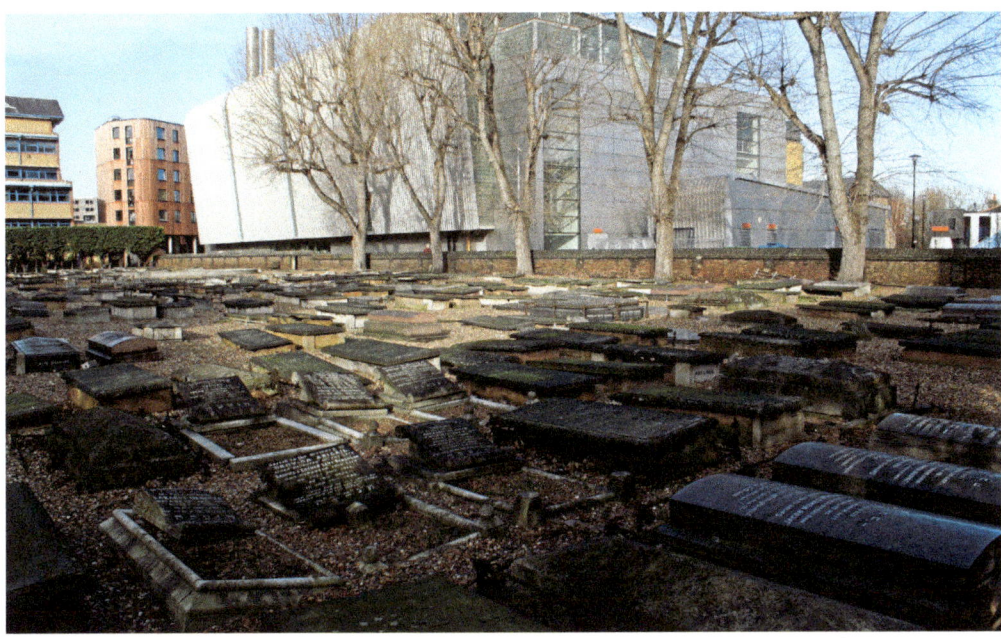

The Novo Velho Cemetery situated on the Queen Mary College campus, Mile End Road. (Photograph by R. Bard)

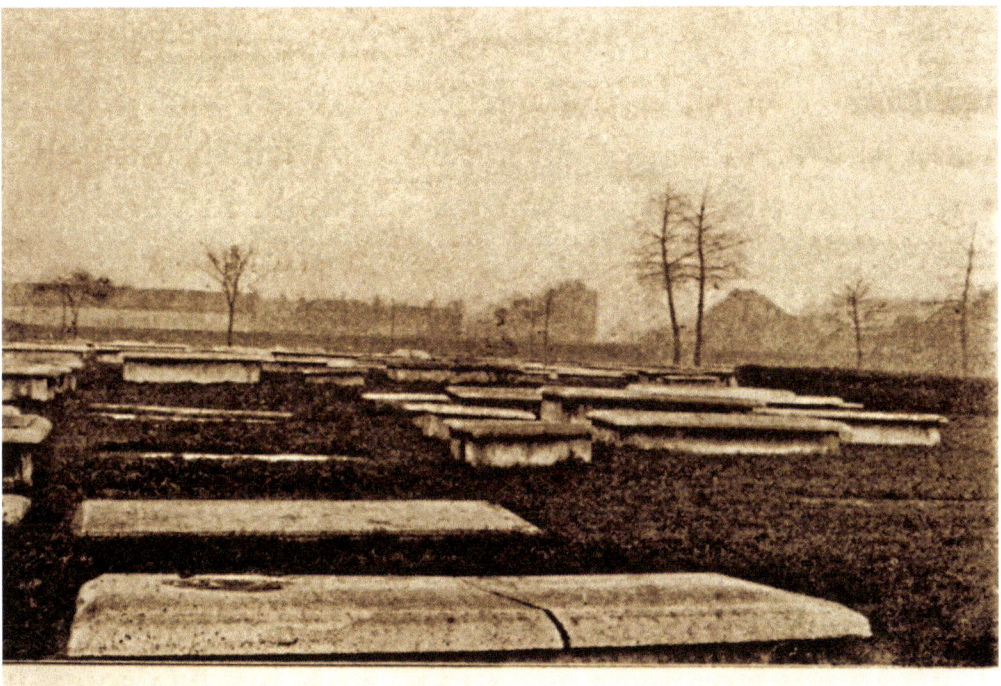

The Jewish Burial Ground, now on the Queen Mary campus, Mile End. (Photograph by Holmes, 1896)

Bibliography

Black, G. D. (2003). *Jewish London: An Illustrated History*. Derby, Breedon.

Brickley, M, and Miles, A, with Stainer, H, 1999, The Cross Bones Burial Ground, Redcross Way, Southwark, London, MoLAS Monograph 3

Barber B. and C. Thomas, 2002, The London Charterhouse, MOLA Monograph.

Connell, B, and Miles, A, 2010 The City Bunhill Burial Ground, Golden Lane: Excavations at South Islington Schools, 2006 MOLA Archaeology studies series 21, London

Commission, E. P. L. and E. S. K. C. B. Chadwick Report to Her Majesty's Principal Secretary of State for the Home Department, from the Poor Law Commissioners, on an inquiry into the sanitary condition of the labouring population of Great Britain; with appendices. [Compiled by E. Chadwick.] (Report on the Sanitary Condition of the Labouring Population of Great Britain. A Supplementary Report on the results of a special inquiry into the practice of interment in towns. Made at the request of Her Majesty's Principal Secretary of State for the Home Department, by E. Chadwick. -Sanitary Inquiry.-England. Local Reports, etc.-Sanitary Inquiry: -Scotland. Reports, etc.), 4 pt. London, 1842.

Defoe, D. and L. A. Landa (1990). A journal of the plague year: being observations or memorials of the most remarkable occurrences as well public as private, which happened in London during the last great visitation in 1665: written by a citizen who continued all the while in London. Oxford, Oxford University Press.

Evelyn, J., E. S. De Beer, et al. (2006). *The Diary of John Evelyn*, London, Everyman's Library.

Fowler, L and Powers, N, 2014, Doctors, dissection and resurrection men, MOLA Monograph 62

Gavin, H. *Sanitary Ramblings; Being Sketches and Illustrations of Bethnal Green. A Type of the Condition of the Metropolis and Other Large Towns*, London, 1848.

Hackman, H. (1981). Wates's Book of London Churchyards: A Guide to the Old Churchyards and Burial-Grounds of the City and Central London. London, Collins.

Harding, V. (1993). "Burial of the plague dead in early modern London." *Epidemic Disease in London*: 53-64.

Harding, V. (2002). *The dead and the living in Paris and London, 1500-1670*, Cambridge, Cambridge University Press.

Henderson, M, Miles, A, and Ritchie, S, in prep, Burial grounds and poorhouses: three post-medieval burial grounds in the parish of St James, *Westminster: Excavations at Marshall Street*, London W1, 2008–9, MOLA Monograph Series, London

Henderson, M, Miles, A, and Walker, D, 2013,'He being dead yet speaketh'. *Excavations at Three Post-medieval Burial Grounds in Tower Hamlets, East London, 2004–2008*, MOLA Monograph Series, London

Henderson, M, Miles, A, and Walker, D 2015 The Paddington Street burial ground of St Marylebone parish: *Excavations at Paddington Street, 2012-3*, MOLA Arch Studies Series

Hill. Frere (1890). *Memorials of Stepney Parish*, Guildford, Billing.

Holmes, I. M. (1896). *The London Burial Grounds. Notes on Their History from the Earliest Times to the Present Day* ... Illustrated. London, T. F. Unwin.

Howarth, G. and P. Jupp (1997). *The Changing Face of Death: Historical Accounts of Death and Disposal*, Basingstoke, Macmillan.

Kent, W. t. c. (1947). *The Lost treasures of London*, [S.l.], Phoenix House.

Knight, C. (1841). *London*, [S.l.], Charles Knight & Co.

Mackinder, A. (2000). *A Romano-British Cemetery on Watling Street: Excavations at 165 Great Dover Street, Southwark, London*, [London], Museum of London Archaeology Service.

Maitland, W. F. R. S. (1739). The History of London from its foundation by the Romans to the present time ... With the several accounts of Westminster, Middlesex, Southwark, and other parts within the Bill of Mortality, London.

Miles, A, with Connell, B, 2012 New Bunhill Fields burial ground, Southwark: Excavations at Globe Academy, 2008 MOLA Archaeology studies series 24, London

Miles, A and Bekvalac, J, 2014, Excavations at Royal Mint Square London Archaeologist vol 14, No 2, 31-36

Miles, A, Powers, N and Wroe-Brown, R, 2008 St Marylebone Church and burial ground: Excavations at St Marylebone School, 1993 and 2004–6, MoLAS Monograph Series 46, London

Miles, A, and White, W, with Tankard, D, 2008 Burial at the site of the parish church of St Benet Sherehog before and after the Great Fire, MoLAS Monograph Series 39, London

Meteyard, E. (1861). The Hallowed Spots of Ancient London. Historical, biographical and antiquarian sketches, illustrative of places and events made memorable by the struggles of our forefathers for civil and religious freedom, London, 1862.

Page, W. R. A. *The Victoria History of London, including London within the Bars, Westminster & Southwark*, 1909-.

Pennant, T. (1813). Some account of London, Westminster and Southwark: illustrated with numerous views. London.

Pepys, S., J. Smith, et al. *The diary of Samuel Pepys: Dent*, 1906 (1943).

Richardson, R. (1987), *Death, Dissection and the Destitute*, London, Routledge & Kegan Paul.

Shepherd, T. H. Views and history of London in the nineteenth century: being a series of illustrations ... from original drawings, with historical descriptions from the earliest periods. [S.l.], T. Holmes.

Stanford, (1860). *Stanford's New London Guide*. With two maps, London: 8°.

Stow, J. and H. Morley (1994). *A survey of London: written in the year, 1598*. Stroud, Alan Sutton.

Stow, et al. (1720). A survey of the cities of London and Westminster ... brought down from the year 1633 ... to the present time by J. Strype. To which is prefixed the life of the author by the editor, etc, 2 vol. London.

Timbs, J. (1855). *Curiosities of London: exhibiting the most rare and remarkable objects of interest in the Metropolis*, London.

Thomas, C, 2004, Life and death in London's east End: 2000 years at Spitalfields', Museum of London Archaeology Service

Walker, G. A. (1839). Gatherings from grave-yards: particularly those of London. With a concise history of the modes of interment among different nations ... and a detail of ... results produced by the ... custom of inhuming the dead in the midst of the living, London, Nottingham [printed].

Walker, G. A. (1846). Burial-ground Incendiarism. The last fire at the Bone-House in the Spa-Fields Golgotha, or the minute anatomy of Grave-digging in London, London.

Walker, G A, (1849) The first–fourth of a series of lectures delivered at the Mechanics Institution, Southampton Buildings, Chancery Lane, on the actual condition of the Metropolitan burial grounds, London'

Ziegler, P. (1970). *The Black Death*, Harmondsworth, Penguin.

Probably the most interesting web site on the subject is
http://www.burial.magic-nation.co.uk/